It is not the strongest of the species that survives, nor the most intelligent that survives. It is the one that is the most adaptable to change.

Charles Darwin

LANDMARKS FOR SUSTAINABILITY

Events and initiatives that have changed our world

Written by **Wayne Visser**
on behalf of the **University of Cambridge
Programme for Sustainability Leadership**

Acknowledgements

Research and editorial assistance by **Oliver Dudok van Heel**, Living Values

Editorial review by **Mike Peirce**, **Polly Courtice**, **Margaret Adey** and **Aled Jones**, Cambridge Programme for Sustainability Leadership

Book design by laliabril.com

© 2009 Greenleaf Publishing Ltd

Published by Greenleaf Publishing Limited
Aizlewood's Mill
Nursery Street
Sheffield S3 8GG
UK
www.greenleaf-publishing.com

Printed and bound in the UK by Cambrian Printers Limited, Aberystwyth
Printed on Regency Satin FSC-accredited paper from well-managed forests and other controlled sources

Mixed Sources
Product group from well-managed
forests and other controlled sources
www.fsc.org Cert no. TT-COC-2200
© 1996 Forest Stewardship Council

British Library Cataloguing in Publication Data:
    Landmarks for sustainability : events and initiatives that
    have changed our world
    1. Sustainable development
    I. Cambridge Programme for Industry
    338.9'27

ISBN-13: 9781906093174

Contents

Introduction   7
Polly Courtice, Director, Cambridge Programme for Sustainability Leadership

A GLOBAL CHALLENGES   10

I Environment, health and safety   12

1 State of the planet   14
With spotlights on the WWF Living Planet Index and the UN Millennium
Ecosystem Assessment

2 Crisis events   22
With spotlights on *Exxon Valdez*, Shell Brent Spar and Shell in Nigeria

3 Climate change   30
With spotlights on the Intergovernmental Panel on Climate Change
and the Kyoto Protocol

4 Health and safety   38
With spotlights on OHSAS 18001, 'Big Pharma' and access to AIDS drugs

II Society and economy   46

5 Globalisation and its critics   48
With spotlights on the protests in Seattle and Genoa,
and Live 8 and Make Poverty History

6 Poverty and development   56
With spotlights on the Millennium Development Goals and the Bottom
of the Pyramid (BOP) model

7 Human rights   64
With spotlights on Nike and the UN Norms on Business and Human Rights

8 Corruption and transparency   72
With spotlights on Transparency International's indexes and
the Extractive Industries Transparency Initiative

B GLOBAL RESPONSES   80

III Leadership   82

9 World summits   84
With spotlights on the Rio Earth Summit and the Johannesburg World Summit

10 Business associations   92
With spotlights on the World Business Council for Sustainable Development
and the UN Global Compact

11 Leadership initiatives   100
With spotlights on the World Economic Forum and the World Social Forum

12 Social enterprise   108
With spotlights on Grameen Bank and the Schwab and Skoll Foundations

IV Collaboration   116

13 Industry initiatives   118
With spotlights on Responsible Care and the Forest Stewardship Council

14 Financial initiatives   126
With spotlights on the UNEP Finance Initiative and the Equator Principles

15 Sustainable investment   134
With spotlights on sustainability indexes and clean-tech investment

16 Sustainable consumerism   142
With spotlights on eco-labelling and fairtrade

V Management   150

17 Codes and standards   152
With spotlights on ISO 14001 and SA8000

18 Corporate governance   160
With spotlights on Enron's collapse and the King Report on Corporate Governance

19 Sustainability reporting   168
With spotlights on the Global Reporting Initiative and the Carbon Disclosure Project

20 Stakeholder engagement   176
With spotlights on McDonald's (McLibel and *Super Size Me*) and AccountAbility
(AA1000 and Responsible Competitiveness Index)

Conclusion   184
Mike Peirce, Deputy Director, Cambridge Programme for Sustainability Leadership

Landmarks timeline   186

About the author   198

About CPSL   199

Introduction

Behind every book, there is always a story — something that sparked the original idea. In the case of *Landmarks*, it was more a confluence of ideas and timing. As the Cambridge Programme for Sustainability Leadership prepared to celebrate its 20th anniversary in 2008, we found ourselves reflecting on what we were celebrating and how we might view the challenges that lay ahead. We found much to celebrate in how far the sustainability agenda has moved in just two decades.

However, in looking at the challenges that lie ahead, we were struck by the sobering prospect of how much more there is to do, and at the same time by a sense of optimism that all is not lost — that so much can be achieved by a relatively small number of dedicated and committed individuals.

In working with hundreds of leaders from business, the public sector and civil society from around the world, we have been inspired by the genuine desire of so many of them to do the right thing, and by their growing openness to the need for transformational change.

So this book is in part an answer to our question: How did we come so far in such a short time, and is it still a case of 'too little, too late'?

Back in 1988, the Brundtland Commission had only just introduced its touchstone definition of sustainable development and all the talk was of the ozone hole, with climate change still something that most people didn't know or care too much about, despite the Intergovernmental Panel on Climate Change (IPCC) being set up by the UN that same year.

Fast-forward to 2008 and we are awash with codes of conduct, certifiable standards, corporate programmes, industry initiatives, green politicians, triple-bottom-line reports and Oscar-winning documentaries about sustainability. At the same time, many of the global challenges — be they climate change, water depletion, biodiversity loss, bribery and corruption or income inequality — seem if anything to be getting worse rather than better.

Which leads to the second question that served as a catalyst for this book, namely: How can we deepen our understanding of the processes of change — at a societal, sector, organisational and individual level — and how have these acted either in support of, or in opposition to, sustainability? In fact, these are the same issues and questions CPSL has been wrestling with over the past 20 years in its executive education programmes, and it seemed to make sense to capture some of that learning in a publication.

The book illustrates a number of trends:

- It is clear that many of the issues highlighted in the next 20 chapters have moved from the marginal fringes into the mainstream. For example, although the UK Soil Association introduced its organic label in 1967, it took until 2004 before Wal-Mart converted to organic cotton supplies and changed the market irrevocably.

- We have seen a move from general problems to specific solutions. For example, we now talk less about environment, poverty and sustainable development and more about ISO 14001, the Millennium Development Goals and emissions trading. Twenty years ago, the call was for more data and debate; today, it is for more policy and action.

- Business and government has changed from being largely reactive to more proactive. For example, the reaction by the chemicals industry to Rachel Carson's *Silent Spring* in the 1960s, Greenpeace's activism in the 1970s and the spate of industrial disasters in the 1980s stands in stark contrast to the approach taken by the Forest Stewardship Council in the 1990s and the Corporate Leaders Group on Climate Change in the 2000s.

- We have also shifted from high-level cross-sector principles to more detailed industry-sector responses. For example, the Sullivan Principles in 1977, the Valdez Principles (now the Ceres Principles) in 1989 and the International Chamber of Commerce (ICC) Business Charter for Sustainable Development in 1991 have given way to the likes of the Marine Stewardship Council (MSC) certification scheme, the Equator Principles for project finance and the Extractive Industries Transparency Initiative.

- Finally, we have seen a growing consensus on principles and standards. The initial flurry of codes and guidelines seem to have settled around a few core standards, such as the Global Reporting Initiative's Sustainability Reporting Guidelines, the UN Global Compact and Millennium Development Goals, the World Resources Institute's Greenhouse Gas Protocol and the UN Principles for Responsible Investment.

Looking at the events thematically, we notice that change is a long-term process, but sustained momentum is important to reach the necessary tipping points in public opinion, policy response and business action. For example, the global warming greenhouse effect was first discovered by Jean-Baptiste Fourier in 1824, but it is only really in the last three years that climate change has become a top agenda item for the news desks, parliaments and boardrooms of the world.

Likewise, the process of institutionalising globalisation may have begun with the formation of the League of Nations in 1919 and marched behemoth-like onward with Bretton Woods in 1944 and GATT and WTO into the 1990s, but it took the 'Battle of Seattle' in 1999 and subsequent 'anti-globalisation' protests to reopen the debate on what kinds of globalisation and capitalism will create a just and sustainable world.

This book helps tell the story of gathering momentum and shifting agendas. Its message in many ways is simple: the last 20 years have been critical — with significant and increasing responses by business, government and civil society. But all the signs are that our social and environmental problems continue to get worse. So, the next 20 years will be even more important — especially with the narrow 'window of opportunity' on climate change, poverty alleviation and sustainable development paths for China, India and other developing countries.

The quality of the leadership that we experience and that we offer will determine whether we take the right path as a species — the path to breakdown or the path to breakthrough. Our work at the Cambridge Programme for Sustainability Leadership is based on the belief that breakthrough is possible and that there is everything to play for by devoting our efforts towards working with leaders who are in a position to effect that transformation.

Polly Courtice, *Director, University of Cambridge Programme for Sustainability Leadership*

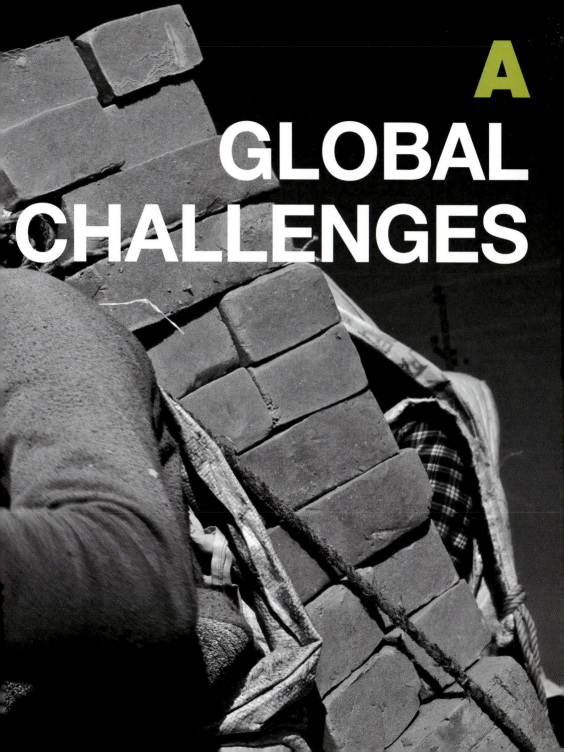

A
GLOBAL CHALLENGES

ENVIRONMENT, HEALTH AND SAFETY

1
STATE OF THE PLANET

Ecosystems are capital assets. We don't include them on our balance sheets, but if we did the services they supply would dwarf everything else in value. Ecosystems support human life, and by harming them we harm ourselves.

TAYLOR RICKETTS, **Director of the Conservation Science Program, WWF**

The Millennium Ecosystem Assessment confirms what the environmental movement has been saying for decades: protecting our planet and its resources is not a special interest, but a human interest.

PETER SELIGMANN, **Chairman and CEO of Conservation International**

There was once a town in the heart of America where all life seemed to live in harmony with its surroundings . . . Then a strange blight crept over the area and everything began to change . . . There was a strange stillness . . . The few birds seen anywhere were moribund; they trembled violently and could not fly. It was a spring without voices. On the mornings that had once throbbed with the dawn chorus of scores of bird voices there was now no sound; only silence lay over the fields and woods and marsh.

RACHEL CARSON, in *Silent Spring*

Ecosystem degradation is highly relevant to business because companies not only impact ecosystems and the services they provide but also depend on them. Ecosystem degradation, therefore, can pose a number of risks to corporate performance as well as create new business opportunities.

WBCSD and WRI, *The Corporate Ecosystem Services Review*

Assessing the web of life on which we depend...

Assessing the 'state of the planet' has been a 50-year process of continuous improvement, in terms of the quantity and quality of data available to build up a comprehensive and reliable picture. Among the first to begin systematically collecting data was the World Conservation Union (IUCN), which launched its Red List of Threatened Species in 1963, and today includes information on more than 40,000 species.

Perhaps the first to look systemically at the planet's economic, social and environmental interactions and trends was the Club of Rome, which published its *Limits to Growth* report in 1972. The authors built a world model that investigated accelerating industrialisation, rapid population growth, widespread malnutrition, depletion of non-renewable resources, and a deteriorating environment. Although the prediction of a 'sudden and uncontrollable decline' within 50–80 years was controversial at the time, their 30-year update published in 2004 reaches a very similar conclusion.

The challenge of regularly tracking and reporting on a range of planetary indicators was taken up by the Worldwatch Institute, which published its first *State of the World* report in 1984 and *Vital Signs* in 1992. The *State of the World* report focused on changes in land, water, energy and biological support systems and their effect on the economy, while *Vital Signs* included social indicators such as food production, infant mortality, cigarette smoking, military expenditure and Third World debt.

Other similar global assessments followed, with the World Resources Institute publishing its first *World Resources* report in 1986, the United Nations Environment Programme (UNEP) its first *Global Environment Outlook* (*GEO-1*) report in 1987 and WWF its first *Living Planet Report* in 1998. One of the powerful features of the WWF report is that it shows humanity's ecological footprint and the Earth's biocapacity country by country and for the world as a whole.

A joint project by Yale and Columbia Universities in 2000 went further to calculate an Environmental Sustainability Index as a basis for ranking countries, with Norway topping the list and Uganda performing worst. They also launched an Environmental Performance Index in 2006, with Switzerland topping the list of 149 countries in 2008 and Niger coming bottom.

The most comprehensive assessment of the state of the planet to date is the Millennium Ecosystem Assessment (MEA), called for by UN Secretary-General Kofi Annan in 2000, initiated in 2001 and completed in 2005. With a budget of US$24 million, the MEA synthesised the findings of over 1,300 scientists to report on the state of 24 ecosystem services, concluding that 60% have already been degraded.

As our knowledge of the state of the planet has improved, denial is no longer a credible position. We now have evidence of the scale of our human impacts, the seriousness of our predicament and the urgency for action.

1963	IUCN Red List first published
1970	Base year for the Living Planet Index
1984	*State of the World* first published by the Worldwatch Institute
1986	*World Resources* first published by the World Resources Institute
1992	*Vital Signs* first published by the Worldwatch Institute
1997	*Global Environment Outlook* first published by the UN Environment Programme (UNEP)
1998	*Living Planet Report* first published by WWF
2000	Environmental Sustainability Index first published
2005	Millennium Ecosystem Assessment published
2006	Environmental Performance Index first published

WWF Living Planet Index

The Living Planet Index was originally developed in 1997 by WWF in collaboration with the UN Environment Programme World Conservation Monitoring Centre. UNEP-WCMC collected much of the data for the index in the first few years of the project.

The Index measures trends in the Earth's biological diversity. Separate indexes are produced for terrestrial, marine and freshwater species, and the three trends are then averaged to create an aggregated index. Although vertebrates represent only a fraction of known species, it is assumed that trends in their populations are typical of biodiversity overall.

By tracking wild species, the Living Planet Index is also monitoring the health of ecosystems. This global trend suggests that we are degrading natural ecosystems at a rate unprecedented in human history.

WWF also measures the 'ecological footprint' for the world and each country, which measures humanity's demand on the biosphere in terms of the area of biologically productive land and sea required to provide the resources we use and to absorb our waste.

This is compared to the Earth's 'biocapacity', which is the amount of biologically productive area — cropland, pasture, forest and fisheries — that is available to meet humanity's needs.

FACTBOX

▶ The Index tracks over 6,000 populations of 1,313 vertebrate species — fish, amphibians, reptiles, birds, mammals — from all around the world, including 695 terrestrial, 274 marine and 344 freshwater species.

▶ Between 1970 and 2003, the overall Living Planet Index fell by 29%. The Terrestrial Index fell by 31%, the Marine Index fell by 27% and the Freshwater Index fell by 28%.

▶ Humanity's ecological footprint has more than tripled since 1961. Since the late 1980s, we have been in overshoot — the world's ecological footprint has exceeded the Earth's biocapacity — as of 2003 by about 25%.

▶ Climate-changing emissions now make up 48% — almost half — of our global footprint (in 2006).

▶ In 2003 the global ecological footprint was 14.1 billion global hectares, or 2.2 global hectares per person (a global hectare is a hectare with world-average ability to produce resources and absorb wastes). The total supply of productive area, or biocapacity, in 2003 was 11.2 billion global hectares, or 1.8 global hectares per person.

▶ The USA has the highest ecological footprint at 9.6 global hectares per person, compared with the average of 2.2, the sustainable level of 1.8 and the lowest (of Afghanistan) of 0.1.

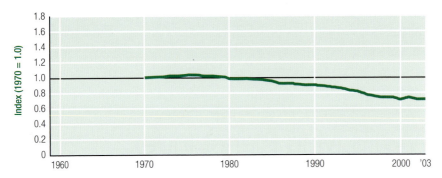

Figure 1 **Living Planet Index, 1970–2003**

Source: WWF, *Living Planet Report 2006*

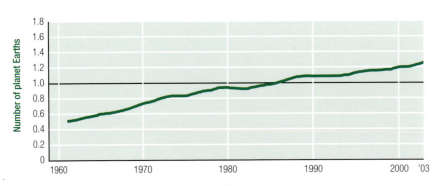

Figure 2 **Humanity's ecological footprint, 1961–2003**

Source: WWF, *Living Planet Report 2006*

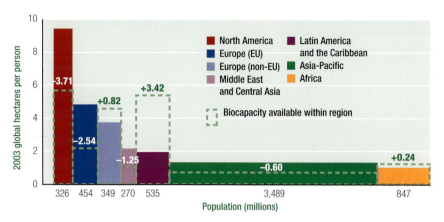

Figure 3 **Ecological footprint and biocapacity by region, 2003**
Source: WWF, *Living Planet Report 2006*

UN Millennium Ecosystem Assessment

The Millennium Ecosystem Assessment (MEA) was commissioned by the United Nations Secretary-General Kofi Annan in 2000. Initiated in 2001, the objective of the MEA was to assess the consequences of ecosystem change for human well-being and the scientific basis for action needed to enhance the conservation and sustainable use of those systems and their contribution to human well-being.

The MEA involved the work of more than 1,360 experts worldwide. Their findings, contained in five technical volumes and six synthesis reports, provide a state-of-the-art scientific appraisal of the condition and trends in the world's ecosystems and the services they provide (such as clean water, food, forest products, flood control and natural resources) and the options to restore, conserve or enhance the sustainable use of ecosystems.

Launched in 2005, the MEA found that, over the past 50 years, humans have changed ecosystems more rapidly and extensively than in any comparable period of time in human history, largely to meet rapidly growing demands for food, freshwater, timber, fibre and fuel. This has resulted in a substantial and largely irreversible loss in the diversity of life on Earth.

The changes that have been made to ecosystems have contributed to substantial net gains in human well-being and economic development, but these gains have been achieved at growing costs in the form of the degradation of many ecosystem services, increased risks of non-linear changes, and the exacerbation of poverty for some groups of people. These problems, unless addressed, will substantially diminish the benefits that future generations obtain from ecosystems.

FACTBOX

- ▶ Sixty per cent of world ecosystem services have been degraded.
- ▶ Of 24 evaluated ecosystems, 15 are being damaged.
- ▶ About a quarter of the Earth's land surface is now cultivated.
- ▶ People now use between 40% and 50% of all available freshwater running off the land. Water withdrawals have doubled over the past 40 years.
- ▶ Over a quarter of all fish stocks are overharvested.
- ▶ Since 1980, about 35% of mangroves have been lost.
- ▶ About 20% of corals were lost in just 20 years; 20% more have been degraded.
- ▶ Nutrient pollution has led to eutrophication of waters and coastal dead zones.
- ▶ Species extinction rates are now 100–1,000 times above the background rate.

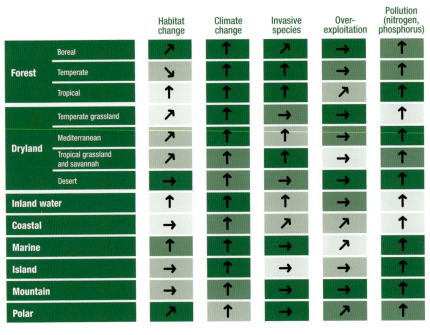

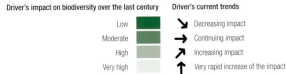

Figure 4 **Impacts on ecosystems**
Source: Millennium Ecosystem Assessment, 2005

BOOKS

Jared Diamond, *Collapse: How Societies Choose to Fail or Survive* (Penguin, 2006)

Donella H. Meadows, Dennis L. Meadows, Jorgen Randers and William W. Behrens III, *The Limits to Growth* (Universe Books, 1972)

Donella H. Meadows, Jorgen Randers and Dennis L. Meadows, *Limits to Growth: The 30-Year Update* (Chelsea Green/Earthscan, 2004)

REPORTS

2008 Environmental Performance Index (Yale Center for Environmental Law and Policy and Columbia University Center for International Earth Science Information Network)

2005 Environmental Sustainability Index: Benchmarking National Environmental Stewardship (Yale Center for Environmental Law and Policy and Columbia University Center for International Earth Science Information Network)

Global Environment Outlook: Environment for Development (GEO-4) (United Nations Environment Programme [UNEP], 2007)

A Global Species Assessment (2004) (World Conservation Union [IUCN])

Living Planet Report 2006 (WWF)

Millennium Ecosystem Assessment Synthesis Report (Millennium Ecosystem Assessment [MEA] and World Resources Institute [WRI], 2005)

State of the World 2008: Innovations for a Sustainable Economy (Worldwatch Institute)

Vital Signs 2007–2008 (Worldwatch Institute)

World Resources Report 2008. Roots of Resilience: Growing the Wealth of the Poor (World Resources Institute [WRI])

WEBSITES

Club of Rome: www.clubofrome.org

Environmental Performance Index: sedac.ciesin.columbia.edu/es/epi

Environmental Sustainability Index: sedac.ciesin.columbia.edu/es/esi and www.yale.edu/esi

IUCN Red List: www.iucnredlist.org

Millennium Ecosystem Assessment: www.millenniumassessment.org

UNEP Global Environment Outlook: www.unep.org/geo

World Resources Institute (WRI): www.wri.org

WRI Earthtrends: earthtrends.wri.org

WRI World Resources: www.wri.org/project/world-resources

Worldwatch Institute: www.worldwatch.org

WWF Living Planet Index and Report: www.panda.org/news_facts/publications/living_planet_report/living_planet_index

2
CRISIS EVENTS

Victims have the right to be heard in court, and multinational companies shouldn't be able to skip town or hide behind subsidiaries or mergers. This case [Bhopal] tragically demonstrates that transnational companies need to be better regulated to eliminate corporate complicity in human rights abuses.

AMNESTY INTERNATIONAL

One thing is certain. The days when companies were judged solely in terms of economic performance and wealth creation have disappeared. For us, Brent Spar was the key turning point. It was a wake-up call, not only to Shell, but to the entire oil and gas industry, and to industry in general.

MALCOLM BRINDED, former Shell UK Country Chairman

The company has suffered enough and spent billions to restore the water quality and beaches. This was not an intentional act. It was not malicious. The company did not stand to make one dollar of profit.

WALTER DELLINGER, Exxon legal representative

The Ogoni have been gradually ground to dust by the combined effort of the multi-national oil company, Shell Petroleum Development Company, the murderous ethnic majority in Nigeria and the country's military dictatorships.

KEN SARO-WIWA, Nigerian human rights activist

Water canno
sprayed on Sh
disused oil installat
Brent Spar to prev
Greenpe
transferring supp
to activists occupy
the S
© Greenpeace/David

When it all goes horribly wrong…

Between 1830 and 2000, 716 mining accidents in the United States killed 15,183 people. However, it tends to be the large, controversial accidents that capture the headlines and are remembered by history.

Perhaps the first of these was the 1976 Seveso disaster — an explosion at the ICMESA chemical plant on the outskirts of Meda, a small town about 20 km north of Milan, Italy, releasing a toxic cloud containing the TCDD dioxin. Although there were no human fatalities, around 450 people suffered skin lesions, 3,300 animals died and an additional 80,000 had to be slaughtered. This later resulted in the introduction of a set of EU industrial safety regulations called the Seveso Directive in 1982.

Another of the world's worst industrial disasters happened in 1984, when an explosion at Union Carbide's pesticide plant in Bhopal, India, released a cloud of methyl isocyanate, killing at least 2,000 and injuring 50,000. Other tragedies include the 1966 Aberfan mining disaster in Wales which killed 148 people, the toy factory fire near Bangkok in Thailand in 1993 which killed 188 workers, and the oil pipe explosion in Jesse, Nigeria, which killed more than 1,000 people in 1998.

Nuclear accidents, especially during the height of the Cold War, have been especially controversial, from the Three Mile Island nuclear disaster in the USA in 1979, where over 140,000 people were evacuated within a 15-mile area, to the Chernobyl nuclear meltdown in the Ukraine in 1986, which resulted in 56 direct deaths and an estimated 4,000 additional fatalities due to cancer from exposure to radiation.

Thankfully, deaths from large-scale industrial disasters have diminished over the past 20 years, although impacts remain serious. For example, in China in 2004, a gas explosion in Daping coal mine in Henan province killed 56 people.

The other type of industrial accident that has shaped the sustainability agenda over the past 20 years is the environmental disaster. The first to focus world attention was the leaking of more than 30 tons of toxic chemicals from the Sandoz chemical plant in Basel into the Rhine in 1986, which killed half a million fish and endangered drinking water supplies.

Another was the spillage of 40 million litres of crude oil by the *Exxon Valdez* tanker off the coast of Alaska in 1989, leading to widespread ecological destruction. The accident led to the creation of the Valdez Principles (now the Ceres Principles) and changes in the oil transportation industry, such as the introduction of double-hulled tankers by 2015.

Other high-profile environmental catastrophes include the sinking of the *Erika* oil tanker off the Brittany coast in 1999 and the Petrobras P36 oil platform off Brazil in 2001. As a response to this litany of disasters, companies have invested significantly over the past 20 years in health and safety and emergency response management systems in an attempt reduce the risks and impacts.

Greenpeace survey of oil pollution in Prince William Sound, Alaska, USA, as a result of the *Exxon Valdez* oil spill
© Greenpeace/Robert Visser

1976	Chemical explosion at ICMESA chemical plant near Seveso (Italy)
1979	Three Mile Island nuclear power plant accident in the USA
1984	Union Carbide gas leak in Bhopal (India)
1986	Sandoz chemical spill into the Rhine in Basel (Switzerland)
1986	Chernobyl nuclear plant disaster in the Ukraine
1989	*Exxon Valdez* oil spill off Alaskan coast
1991	Petrobras P36 oil platform sinks off Brazilian coast
1995	Shell Brent Spar and Nigeria crises
1998	Oil pipeline explosion at Jesse (Nigeria)
2004	Gas explosion in Daping coal mine in Henan province in China

Exxon Valdez oil spill

On 12 March 1989, the *Exxon Valdez* oil tanker ran aground on Bligh Reef, spilling its crude oil cargo into Prince William Sound, an area off the coast of Alaska.

The disaster directly led to the 1990 federal Oil Pollution Act, which seeks to diminish the environmental consequence of spills, and it prompted changes in industry safety standards and emergency response planning. Among the reforms is the introduction of double-hulled tankers by 2015.

It also led to the establishment of the Valdez Principles (now the Ceres Principles) — a 10-point code of corporate environmental conduct to be publicly endorsed by companies as an environmental mission statement or ethic. Over 50 companies have endorsed the Ceres Principles including 13 *Fortune* 500 firms.

Much of the environment has recovered to its pre-spill condition. Among the animal species that have not recovered are common loons, harbour seals, harlequin ducks and Pacific herring.

Today, the *Exxon Valdez* disaster no longer ranks among the top 50 largest oil spills around the world.

FACTBOX

- ▶ The *Exxon Valdez*, carrying 53 million gallons (200 million litres) of crude oil, ruptured 8 of its 11 tanks, spilling 40 million litres which eventually affected 2,250 km of shoreline.
- ▶ Scientists estimate mass mortalities of 1,000–2,800 sea otters, 302 harbour seals, and unprecedented numbers of seabird deaths estimated at 250,000 in the days immediately after the spill.
- ▶ Various economic studies funded by the State of Alaska estimate the economic losses from recreational fishing could be anything between $3.6 million and $630.5 million, and placed a value to the public of a pristine Prince William Sound at $4.9–7.2 billion.
- ▶ The subsequent clean-up over four summers involved at its peak some 10,000 workers, 1,000 boats and 100 aircraft.
- ▶ Exxon claims to have spent $2.1 billion on the clean-up in the years since the spill.
- ▶ Exxon has paid more than $1 billion to state and federal governments for criminal and civil damages.
- ▶ The courts awarded $5 billion in punitive damages to commercial fishermen of Cordova and other affected communities for the economic losses they had incurred as a result of the spill. Exxon is still fighting this award and has succeeded in reducing it to $2.5 billion.
- ▶ ExxonMobil's profits for 2006 were U$39.5 billion, the highest ever for a US company.

Shell Brent Spar and Nigeria

Shell Brent Spar

In 1994, following extensive decommissioning studies, Shell decided to dispose of its Brent Spar oil platform through 'deep-sea disposal' (i.e. sinking it) in the north Atlantic.

In April 1995, Greenpeace occupied the platform to protest against the method of disposal, which they believed was environmentally harmful. Their campaign resulted in mounting international protests and boycotts, including from some European governments.

After three months, and despite the support of the British government, Shell announced that it would not sink Brent Spar, and after a broad engagement process called 'The Way Forward', announced in September 1998 that it would use the platform as a Norwegian Ro/Ro ferry quay.

In July 1998, all the governments of the north-east Atlantic region agreed to ban future dumping of steel-built oil installations. However, with Greenpeace having admitted to misrepresenting some of the facts about the volume of oil on board Brent Spar, the debate about the whether the best environmental interests were served in the Brent Spar case continue to be hotly debated.

Shell in Nigeria

Shell's experiences in Nigeria show that it isn't always exclusively environmental issues that catalyse a crisis, nor is it only when the company is directly involved in an incident.

In the 1990s tensions arose between the native Ogoni people of the Niger Delta and Shell. The concerns of the locals were that very little of the money earned from oil on their land was getting to the people who live there, and that there were significant environmental damages caused by Shell's practices.

In 1993 the Movement for the Survival of the Ogoni People (MOSOP) organised a large protest against Shell and the government. Shell withdrew its operations from the Ogoni areas but the Nigerian government raided their villages and arrested some of the protest leaders.

Some of these arrested protesters, Ken Saro-Wiwa being the most prominent, were tried for murder (which they denied) and were executed in November 1995, despite a plea by Shell for clemency and widespread opposition from the Commonwealth of Nations and international human rights and environmental activists.

Despite Shell's opposition to the executions, there were widespread perceptions of their complicity with the government, which resulted in sustained international protests and boycotts. In 2002, close relatives of Ken Saro-Wiwa also won the right to bring a case against Royal Dutch Shell in the US.

After 1995, Shell began implementing extensive policy reforms, including increased stakeholder engagement and community support and improved performance reporting on social and environmental issues, both in Nigeria and internationally.

xon Valdez oil spill
aster clean-up
Greenpeace

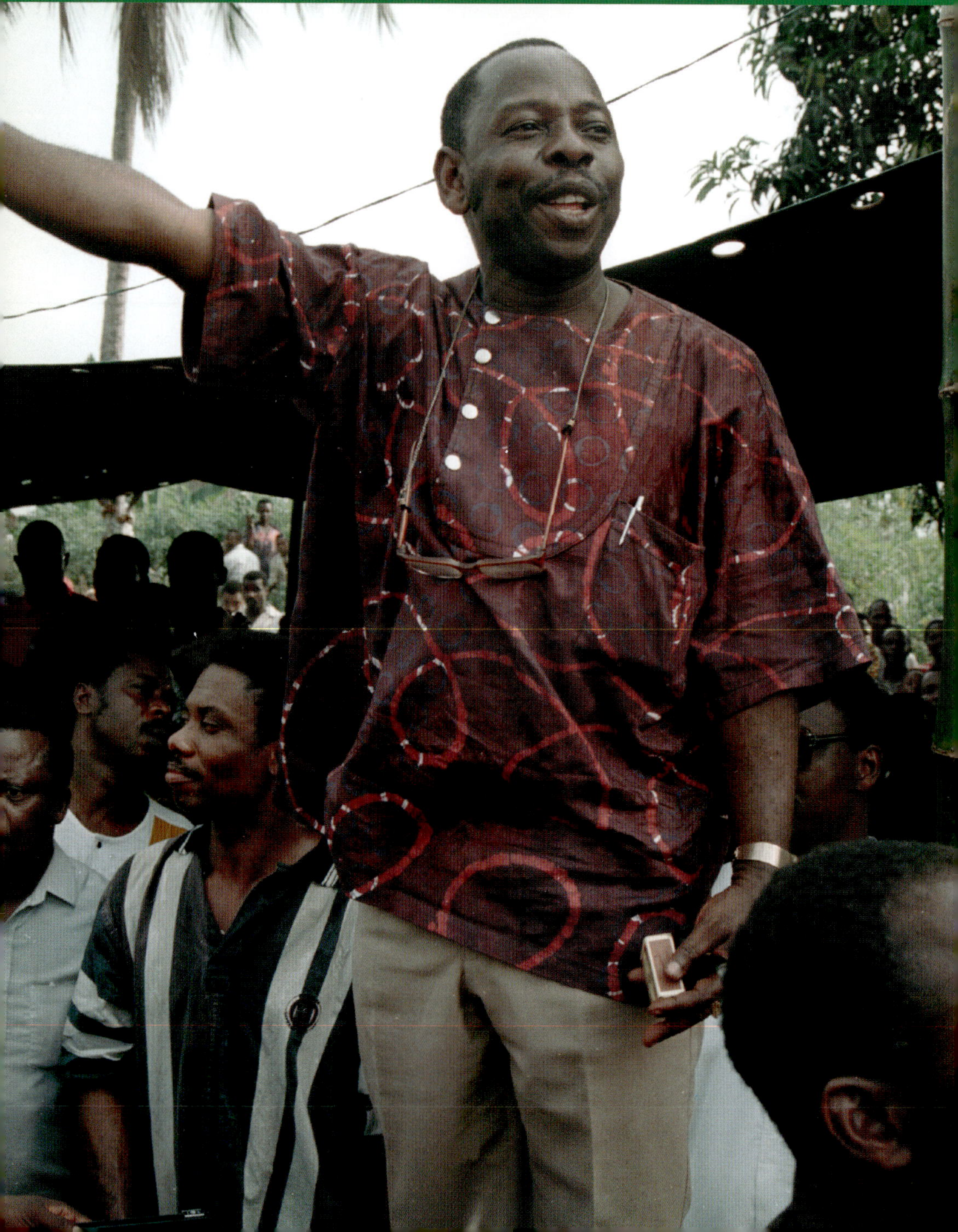

BOOKS

Meena Ahmed, *The Principles and Practice of Crisis Management: The Case of Brent Spar* (Palgrave Macmillan, 2006)

Gil Chandler and Thomas Streissguth, *The Exxon Valdez: The Oil Spill off the Alaskan Coast* (Capstone Press, 2000; Edge Books, 2002)

Themistocles D'Silva, *The Black Box of Bhopal: A Closer Look at the World's Deadliest Industrial Disaster* (Trafford Publishing, 2006)

Dominique Lapierre and Javier Moro, *Five Past Midnight in Bhopal: The Epic Story of the World's Deadliest Industrial Disaster* (Warner Books, 2002)

Gerry McCusker, *Talespin. Public Relations Disasters: Inside Stories and Lessons Learnt* (Kogan Page, 2004)

Ike Okonta, Oronto Douglas and George Monbiot, *Where Vultures Feast: Shell, Human Rights and Oil* (Verso Books, 2003)

Riki Ott, *Sound Truth and Corporate Myth$: The Legacy of the Exxon Valdez Oil Spill* (Dragonfly Sisters Press, 2005)

Victoria Parker, *Chernobyl 1986* (Raintree, 2006)

Tony Rice and Paula Owen, *Decommissioning the Brent Spar* (E&FN Spon, 1999)

Brian Toft and Simon Reynolds, *Learning from Disasters: A Management Approach* (Perpetuity Press, rev. edn, 2005)

J.S. Walker, *Three Mile Island: A Nuclear Crisis in Historical Perspective* (University of California Press, rev. edn, 2006)

WEBSITES

Chernobyl Info: www.chernobyl.info

Dickinson College's Three Mile Island website: www.threemileisland.org

Exxon Community and Society website: www.exxonmobil.com/Corporate/community.aspx

Exxon Valdez Oil Spill Trustee Council: www.evostc.state.ak.us

Human Rights Watch: www.hrw.org

NOAA's Office of Response and Restoration: response.restoration.noaa.gov

Sandoz Social Responsibility website: www.sandoz.com/site/en/social_responsibility/index.shtml

Seveso II Directive: ec.europa.eu/environment/seveso/index.htm

Shell Brent Spar dossier: www.shell.com/home/content/uk-en/about_shell/brentspardossier/dir_brent_spar.html

Shell Environment and Society website: www.shell.com/home/content/envirosoc-en

Shell Nigeria Community and Environment website: www.shell.com/home/content/nigeria/society_environment/dir_community_environment.html

Union Carbide Bhopal Information Centre: www.bhopal.com

3
CLIMATE CHANGE

I worry about climate change. It's the only thing that I believe has the power to fundamentally end the march of civilization as we know it, and make a lot of the other efforts that we're making irrelevant and impossible.

BILL CLINTON, former US President

Climate change is the most severe problem that we are facing today, more serious even than the threat of terrorism.

SIR DAVID KING, former UK government chief scientific adviser

Climate change: it's here. If we don't react, war, pestilence and famine will follow close behind.

R.K. PACHAURI, Chairman, Intergovernmental Panel on Climate Change (IPCC)

If we follow business as usual I can't see how west Antarctica could survive a century. We are talking about a sea-level rise of at least a couple of metres this century . . . What we have found is that the target we have all been aiming for is a disaster — a guaranteed disaster.

JAMES HANSEN, US climate scientist and head of NASA Goddard Institute for Space Studies

Dawes Glacier calvi
from the 200-foot-hi
face: Tongass Natio
Forest, Alaska, US
Nancy Nehring, istockph

Our 'large-scale geophysical experiment' . . .

Scientists have long been aware of the Earth's extreme temperature variations, with the last major ice age ending about 10,000 years ago. However, in 1824 Jean-Baptiste Fourier discovered a global warming (or greenhouse) effect and, in 1861, the Irish physicist John Tyndall carried out key research on carbon dioxide (CO_2) and heat absorption.

In 1896, Swedish and American scientists independently concluded that CO_2 was the likely cause of global warming. By 1957, US oceanographer Roger Revelle was warning that humanity is conducting a 'large-scale geophysical experiment', while colleague David Keeling set up the first continuous monitoring of CO_2 in the atmosphere, confirming year-on-year-rises.

Despite these early signs, it took until 1979 for the first World Climate Conference, organised by the World Meteorological Organisation (WMO), to state that 'continued expansion of man's activities on Earth may cause significant extended regional and even global changes of climate'. This led the WMO and the United Nations Environment Programme (UNEP) to establish a scientific advisory body: the Intergovernmental Panel on Climate Change (IPCC).

The IPCC issued its First Assessment Report in 1990, finding that the planet had warmed by 0.5°C in the past century and would rise further by 0.3°C per decade in the 21st century, accompanied by global mean sea level rises of 6 cm per decade.

1979	First World Climate Conference
1988	Intergovernmental Panel on Climate Change (IPCC) established
1990	1st IPCC report finds 0.5°C warming
1992	UN Framework Convention on Climate Change (UNFCCC) signed
1995	2nd IPCC report predicts significant socioeconomic impacts
1997	Kyoto Protocol sets targets for 34 major economies
2001	3rd IPCC report shows rising temperatures and sea levels
2005	EU GHG Emission Trading Scheme begins trading
2006	Stern Review on Economics of Climate Change published
2007	4th IPCC report shows 90% certainty of human cause of climate change

Convinced that the world needed a global policy response, the UN established the Framework Convention on Climate Change (UNFCCC), which 154 nations (including the US) signed at the Rio 'Earth Summit' in 1992.

In 1995, the IPCC Second Assessment Report confirmed that concentrations of greenhouse gases (GHGs) were continuing to increase, and that the socioeconomic impacts of climate change were significant, while the UNFCCC began negotiations on an international agreement to limit the emission of GHGs. The result was the Kyoto Protocol, adopted in 1997, which: (1) set mandatory targets for emission reductions for the world's 38 leading economies, and (2) proposed three flexible market mechanisms for achieving these reductions through carbon trading. The targets collectively amounted to a 5.2% global reduction in GHGs from these countries against 1990 levels by 2012.

Despite US opposition to the Protocol, momentum continued to build, with the EU launching its Emission Trading Scheme for CO_2 in 2005. In 2007, the UK's Stern Review, prepared by former World Bank Chief Economist Sir Nicholas Stern, warned that tackling climate change will now cost around 1% of global GDP, whereas the cost of not acting could be between 5% and 20%. Shortly thereafter, the IPCC released its Fourth Assessment Report, concluding with 90% confidence that human activity is causing climate change. It seemed the tide was turning, in no small part thanks to former US Vice-President Al Gore, who received an Oscar for his movie *An Inconvenient Truth*, and a Nobel Prize, shared with the IPCC. This seemed to mark the end of denial and the beginning of urgent global action on climate change.

Intergovernmental Panel on Climate Change (IPCC)

The Intergovernmental Panel on Climate Change (IPCC) was founded in 1988 by the World Meteorological Organisation (WMO) and the United Nations Environment Programme (UNEP).

The IPCC is made up of: (1) *governments*, which set the work programme and accept, adopt and approve the IPCC reports; (2) *scientists*, who contribute to the IPCC reports as authors, contributors and reviewers; and (3) *people*: as a United Nations body, the IPCC work aims for the promotion of the UN human development goals.

The IPCC has a task force on national greenhouse gas inventories and three working groups, on: (1) scientific aspects, (2) the vulnerability of socioeconomic and natural systems, and (3) options for adapting to and mitigating climate change.

The IPCC has issued four main Assessment Reports: in 1990, 1995, 2001 and 2007.

FACTBOX

The IPCC Third Assessment Report in 2001 found that:

▶ Global average surface temperatures rose 0.6°C during the 20th century.

▶ Sea level rose between 0.1 and 0.2 metres during the 20th century.

▶ In the Northern Hemisphere, the increase in temperature in the 20th century was the largest of any century during the past 1,000 years.

▶ In the Northern Hemisphere, the 1990s were the warmest decade since records began in 1861, and 1998 was the warmest year since records began in 1861.

▶ There have been average decreases of about 10% in the extent of snow cover around the world since the late 1960s and global ocean heat content has increased since the late 1950s.

▶ There has been a 40% decline in Arctic sea-ice thickness during late summer to early autumn in recent decades and a slower decline in winter sea-ice thickness.

▶ Northern Hemisphere spring and summer sea-ice extent has decreased by about 10–15% since the 1950s.

The IPCC Fourth Assessment Report in 2007 found that:

▶ Global GHG emissions due to human activities have grown since pre-industrial times, with an increase of 70% between 1970 and 2004.

▶ Most of the observed increase in globally averaged temperatures since the mid-20th century is very likely due to the observed increase in anthropogenic (human-induced) GHG concentrations.

The economic implications of these IPCC findings led the 2007 Stern Review to conclude that the global cost of tackling climate change could now be as little as 1% of global annual GDP, but inaction could result in costs of between 5% and 20%.

The Kyoto Protocol

The Kyoto Protocol is an international policy under the UN Framework Convention on Climate Change (UNFCCC) which commits specified countries to stabilise their greenhouse gas (GHG) emissions.

The Protocol covers six of the most important GHGs: carbon dioxide (CO_2), methane (CH_4), nitrous oxide (N_2O), hydrofluorocarbons (HFCs), perfluorocarbons (PFCs) and sulphur hexafluoride (SF_6).

The Protocol was adopted in 1997 and entered into force in 2005. Most notable among those who had not yet ratified was the United States.

The Protocol sets GHG emission reduction targets, to be achieved by 2012, for 38 developed countries (Annex 1 countries). Developing countries (non-Annex 1 countries) do not have targets.

On average, the GHG targets are equivalent to a 5.2% reduction against a 1990 baseline, but they range from an increase of 10% (Iceland) and 8% (Australia) to a decrease of 7% (USA) and 8% (EU).

There are three flexible market mechanisms for carbon trading between 2008 and 2012 under the Protocol: (1) Emissions Trading, (2) Joint Implementation (JI) and (3) the Clean Development Mechanism (CDM).

Negotiations to replace the Kyoto Protocol after 2012 started in Bali in December 2007.

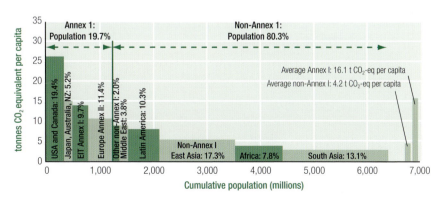

Notes: Year 2004 distribution of regional per capita GHG emissions (all Kyoto gases, including those from land use) over the population of different country groupings. The percentages in the bars indicate a region's share in global GHG emissions. EIT = Economies in Transition

Figure 5 **CO_2 emissions by region (2004)**

Source: IPCC, 2007: Summary for Policymakers. In: *Climate Change 2007: Mitigation. Contribution of Working Group III to the Fourth Assessment Report of the Intergovernmental Panel on Climate Change* [B. Metz, O.R. Davidson, P.R. Bosch, R. Dave, L.A. Meyer (eds.)], Cambridge University Press, Cambridge, United Kingdom and New York, NY, USA.

FACTBOX

- From 1996 to 2005, the GHG emissions for Annex I countries (excluding from land use, land use change and forestry) decreased by 2.8%, although they increased by 2.6% since 2000.
- The UNFCCC estimates that around 2,900 Clean Development Mechanism (CDM) projects under the Kyoto Protocol will generate 2.6 billion Certified Emission Reductions (CERs) by 2012.
- The EU Emission Trading Scheme (EU ETS) — the world's first large-scale emissions trading programme under the Kyoto Protocol — was launched in 2005, covering around 12,000 installations in 25 countries and 6 industrial sectors.
- The carbon market grew to US$30 billion in 2006, three times greater than the previous year. The market was dominated by $25 billion under the EU ETS.
- Project-based activities primarily through the CDM and JI grew sharply to a value of about US$5 billion in 2006. The voluntary market for reductions by corporations and individuals also grew strongly to an estimated US$100 million in 2006.
- New Energy Finance estimates that the US will have a $1 trillion emissions trading market by 2020 if the policy trend towards a cap-and-trade system continues.

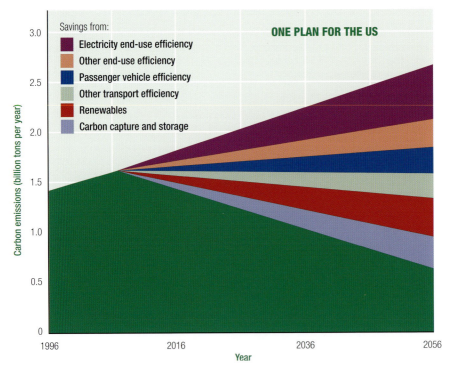

Note: The US share of emissions could, in this Natural Resources Defense Council scenario, be achieved by efficiency gains, renewable energy and clean coal.

Figure 6 'Princeton Wedges': technologies to stabilise climate change

Source: Daniel A. Lashof and David G. Hawkins, Natural Resources Defense Council, in Robert H. Socolow and Stephen W. Pacala, 'A Plan to Keep Carbon in Check', *Scientific American*, September 2006

BOOKS

Al Gore, *An Inconvenient Truth: The Planetary Emergency of Global Warming and What We Can Do About It* (Bloomsbury, 2006)

Jeremy Leggett, *The Carbon War: Global Warming and the End of the Oil Era* (Penguin, 2000)

James Lovelock, *The Revenge of Gaia: Earth's Climate Crisis and the Fate of Humanity* (Basic Books, rev. edn, 2007)

George Monbiot, *Heat: How to Stop the Planet from Burning* (Penguin, new edn, 2007)

REPORTS

A Call for Action (US Climate Action Partnership, 2007)

Cambridge Climate Leaders Reference Guide (University of Cambridge Programme for Sustainability Leadership, 2007)

Carbon Down, Profits Up (The Climate Group, 3rd edn, 2006)

Climate Change 2007: 4th Assessment Report (Physical Science Basis) (IPCC, 2007)

Climate Change and the Greenhouse Effect (The Hadley Centre, 2005)

The Climate Change Challenge: Scientific Evidence and Implications (The Carbon Trust, 2005)

Getting Ahead of the Curve: Corporate Strategies that Address Climate Change (Pew Center on Global Climate Change, 2006)

Limiting Global Climate Change to 2 Degrees Celsius: The Way Ahead for 2020 and Beyond (European Commission, 2007)

Pathways to 2050: Energy and Climate Change (World Business Council for Sustainable Development [WBCSD], 2005)

Stern Review on the Economics of Climate Change (Nicholas Stern and HM Treasury, UK, 2007)

World Energy Outlook 2006 (IEA, 2006)

WEBSITES

BBC, section on climate change: www.bbc.co.uk/climate

Carbon Trust: www.carbontrust.co.uk

Cool Mayors for Climate Protection: www.coolmayors.org

Corporate Leaders Group on Climate Change: www.cpi.cam.ac.uk/bep/clgcc

E3G: www.e3g.org/index.php/programmes/climate

EU Greenhouse Gas Emission Trading Scheme: ec.europa.eu/environment/climat/emission.htm

Institute for Public Policy Research (ippr): www.ippr.org.uk/research/teams/?id=86&tid=86

Intergovernmental Panel on Climate Change (IPCC): www.ipcc.ch

Kyoto Protocol: unfccc.int/kyoto_protocol/items/2830.php

Princeton Stabilization Wedges: www.princeton.edu/~cmi/resources/stabwedge.htm

Stern Review: www.hm-treasury.gov.uk/sternreview_index.htm

Stop Global Warming: www.stopglobalwarming.org

Tyndall Centre for Climate Change Research: www.tyndall.ac.uk

Together.com: www.together.com

Wikipedia on global warming: en.wikipedia.org/wiki/Global_warming

4
HEALTH
AND SAFETY

Purchasing anti-retroviral drugs isn't a cost that's going to kill the company; it's a cost that's going to protect the company.

BRIAN BRINK, Medical Senior Vice President, Anglo American

This court case demonstrates how powerful drug companies are bullying poor countries just so they can protect their patent rights on life-saving medicines.

JUSTIN FORSYTH, Oxfam Policy Director

This is not about profits and patents...We seek no profits on AIDS drugs in Africa, and we will not let our patents be an obstacle.

JOHN L. MCGOLDRICK, Executive Vice President at Bristol-Myers Squibb

I intend to ensure BP becomes an industry leader in process safety management and performance. We will want to do everything possible to prevent another tragedy like the one that occurred at Texas City.

JOHN BROWNE, former CEO, BP

Chemical hazard
Photo

Can you put a price on life and well-being...?

The International Labour Organisation (ILO), established in 1919, has been one of the consistent voices for health and safety in the workplace. In the preamble to its original Constitution, the ILO states one of its goals as 'protection of the worker against sickness, disease and injury arising out of his employment'.

The ILO has since added considerable substance to this general commitment through a range of Conventions, which set out minimum standards and conditions. These include, for example, Conventions on Occupational Hazards (1977), Occupational Safety and Health (1981) and Prevention of Major Industrial Accidents (1993), to mention but a few.

Another UN organisation that has played a strong role in promoting health and safety is the World Health Organisation, established in 1948 by the newly formed United Nations. The day its constitution came into force — 7 April — is now the date celebrated each year as World Health Day.

The UN has also been instrumental in catalysing initiatives, such as UNAIDS, set up in 1996, and the Global Fund to Fight AIDS, Tuberculosis and Malaria (GFATM), proposed by former Secretary-General Kofi Annan in 2001 and launched in 2002. By December 2006, an estimated 1.25 million lives had been saved thanks to the US$3.2 billion of grants disbursed by the GFATM.

However, health and safety has not only been tackled at a multilateral level. Businesses have also invested considerable resources over the years to improving their track record. Until the 1990s, this was largely a reaction to poor public perception and a plethora of legal requirements. However, in the past 20 years, companies have adopted voluntary initiatives, such as OHSAS 18001, launched in 1999, and the Global Business Coalition on HIV/AIDS, established in 2001.

Companies have also made considerable philanthropic contributions to health, such as the US$750 million donated by the Bill & Melinda Gates Foundation in 2000 to set up the Global Fund for Children's Vaccines, as part of the Global Alliance for Vaccines and Immunisation (GAVI).

Despite these initiatives, industry in general, and the pharmaceutical sector in particular, has not been without its critics. This tension was epitomised by the 2001 case of 'Big Pharma' v South Africa, in which 39 pharmaceutical companies tried to block government legislation aimed at increasing access to HIV/AIDS treatment. After widespread national and international protest and severe reputational damage, the companies dropped the case.

The pharmaceutical industry has subsequently responded with extensive donations and numerous programmes to distribute free or cheap HIV/AIDS and other drugs in developing countries. However, the debate around private provision of health products and services still rages, with an almost inevitable conflict between the right of access to health and the need for companies to be profitable.

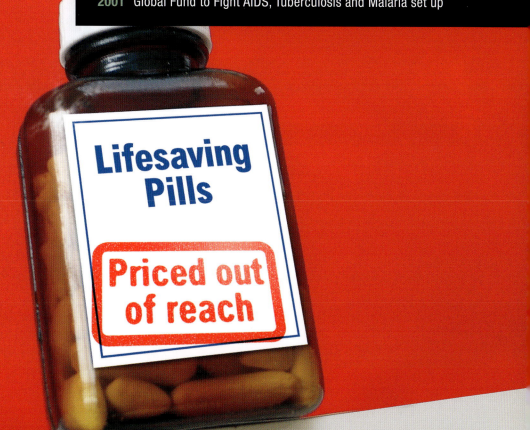

1948	World Health Organisation (WHO) set up by the UN
1977	ILO (International Labour Organisation) Convention on Occupational Hazards issued
1981	ILO Convention on Occupational Safety and Health issued
1993	ILO Convention on Prevention of Major Industrial Accidents issued
1996	UNAIDS established
1999	OHSAS 18001 launched (updated in 2007)
2000	Global Alliance for Vaccines and Immunisation launched
2001	South African Government v Big Pharma court case
2001	Global Business Coalition on HIV/AIDS established
2001	Global Fund to Fight AIDS, Tuberculosis and Malaria set up

Lifesaving Pills

Priced out of reach

OHSAS 18001

OHSAS 18001, published by the British Standards Institution (BSI) in 1999 and updated in 2007, is an Occupational Health & Safety Management System framework standard that allows an organisation to consistently identify and control its health and safety risks, reduce the potential for accidents, aid legislative compliance and improve overall performance.

OHSAS 18001 is specifically designed to be compatible with ISO 9001 and ISO 14001 in order to facilitate the integration of quality, environmental and occupational health and safety management systems.

The following key areas are addressed by OHSAS 18001:

- Planning for hazard identification, risk assessment and risk control
- OHSAS management programme
- Structure and responsibility
- Training, awareness and competence
- Consultation and communication
- Operational control
- Emergency preparedness and response
- Performance measuring, monitoring and improvement.

In September 2005, the American Industrial Hygiene Association (AIHA) released ANSI/AIHA Z10 to replace OHSAS 18001 in the United States as an accredited standard recognised by the American National Standards Institute (ANSI).

FACTBOX

- ▶ According to the ILO, job-related accidents and illnesses annually claim more than 2 million lives, and fatalities are increasing every year.
- ▶ The risk of occupational disease has become by far the most prevalent danger faced by people in their jobs — accounting for 1.7 million annual work-related deaths and outpacing fatal accidents by four to one.
- ▶ By conservative estimates, each year there are 160 million cases of occupational disease (work-related illness) and 270 million occupational accidents in which the victims miss at least three days of work as a result.
- ▶ Workplace accidents and illness are responsible for the loss of around 4% of the world's GDP in compensation and absence from work.
- ▶ In 2004, according to the Associated Press, 6,027 Chinese mine workers were killed — an average of about 16 deaths a day.
- ▶ In the USA, according to the Bureau of Labor Statistics, businesses lose approximately $20 billion annually due to Repetitive Strain Injury (RSI), which accounts for more work time lost than any other work-related injury, averaging 19 days lost per incident.
- ▶ OHSAS 18001 has been adopted in more than 80 countries by approximately 16,000 certified organisations.
- ▶ *Karoshi* is a Japanese word meaning 'death from overwork'.
- ▶ 28 April is the World Day for Safety At Work.

'Big Pharma' and access to AIDS drugs

In 2001, Oxfam launched a campaign called 'Cut the Cost', challenging the pharmaceutical industry to address responsible drug pricing.

In the same year, the Indian pharmaceutical company Cipla cut the annual price of anti-retroviral AIDS drugs to Médecins Sans Frontières (MSF) to $350, as compared with the global industry standard of $1,000, and the Western market price of $10,400.

Cipla also announced its intention to allow the South African government to sell eight of its generic AIDS drugs, the patents for which were held by other companies.

Consequently, MSF put pressure on the five major pharmaceutical companies involved in the UNAIDS Accelerating Access Initiative to match Cipla's benchmark.

Merck's response was to cut the price of its HIV/AIDS treatments for developing countries, including offering Crixivan at $600 and Stocrin at $500.

Pfizer in turn offered to supply antifungal medicine at no charge to HIV/AIDS patients in 50 AIDS-stricken countries.

Bristol-Myers Squibb announced that it would not prevent generic-drug makers from selling low-cost versions of one of its HIV drugs (Zerit) in Africa.

GlaxoSmithKline granted a voluntary licence to South African generics producer Aspen, allowing it to share the rights to GSK's drugs (AZT, 3TC and Combivir) without charge.

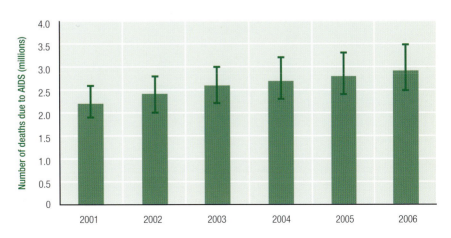

Figure 7 **Estimated number of adult and child (all ages) deaths due to AIDS globally, 2001–2006**

Source: *2006 UNAIDS Annual Report*

However, at the same time, 39 of the largest international pharmaceutical companies took the South African government to court over plans to introduce legislation aimed at easing access to AIDS drugs, arguing that it would infringe their patents and contravene the Trade Related Aspects of Intellectual Property Rights (TRIPS) agreement.

The pharmaceutical companies dropped the case following pressure from the South African government, the European Parliament and 300,000 people from over 130 countries who signed a petition against the action.

FACTBOX

▶ Since 1981, 65 million people have been infected with HIV and 25 million have died of AIDS-related illnesses.
▶ In 2006, 4.3 million new infections were recorded, as were 2.9 million AIDS-related deaths — more than in any previous year.
▶ Today, more than 39.5 million people are living with HIV — half of them women and girls.
▶ Funding levels have increased from some US$300 million in 1996 to US$8.9 billion in 2006.
▶ In 2001, Anglo American estimated that the $4.5 million a year it cost to treat over 50,000 of its employees and their spouses would be offset from savings due to fewer death benefit payouts and less absenteeism.

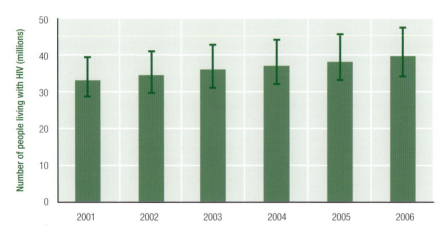

Figure 8 **Estimated number of people living with HIV globally, 2001–2006**
Source: *2006 UNAIDS Annual Report*

REPORTS

A Human Race: Corporate Responsibility Review 2006 (GlaxoSmithKline [GSK], 2001)

Bristol-Myers Squibb 2007 Sustainability Website Contents (Bristol-Myers Squibb, 2007)

The Cape Town Declaration of the Working Alliance for TB Drug Development, 2000

Facing the Challenge: Our Contribution to Improving Healthcare in the Developing World (GlaxoSmithKline [GSK], 2001)

Formula for Fairness: Patient Rights Before Patent Rights (Oxfam, 2001)

ILO Code of Practice on HIV/AIDS and the World of Work (International Labour Organisation [ILO], 2005)

ILO Conventions on Occupational Hazards (No. 148), Occupational Safety and Health (No. 155) and Prevention of Major Industrial Accidents (No. 174) (International Labour Organisation [ILO], 1977, 1981, 1993)

OHSAS 18001: 2007 Occupational Health and Safety Management Systems (BSI British Standards, 2007)

Outstanding Business Action on HIV/AIDS, Tuberculosis and Malaria: Case Studies 2007 (Global Business Coalition on HIV/AIDS)

Pfizer 2007 Corporate Responsibility Report (Pfizer)

Pharma Futures: Prescription for Long-Term Value (SustainAbility, 2007)

UNAIDS Annual Report 2007: Making Money Work

UNAIDS and Business: Working Together (UNAIDS, 2007)

The World Health Report 2007. A Safer Future: Global Public Health Security in the 21st Century (World Health Organisation [WHO])

WEBSITES

Anglo American HIV and AIDS webpage: www.angloamerican.co.uk/cr/hivaids

Bristol-Myers Squibb Corporate Responsibility webpage: www.bms.com/sr

BSI: www.bsi-global.com

Cape Town Declaration: www.tballiance.org/downloads/historical/CapeTownDecl.pdf

GlaxoSmithKline (GSK) Responsibility webpage: www.gsk.com/responsibility

Global Alliance for Vaccines and Immunisation (GAVI): www.gavialliance.org

Global Business Coalition on HIV/AIDS: www.businessfightsaids.org

Global Fund to Fight AIDS, Tuberculosis and Malaria: www.theglobalfund.org

International Labour Organisation (ILO): www.ilo.org

Merck Corporate Responsibility webpage: www.merck.com/cr

Novartis Corporate Citizenship webpage: www.novartis.com/about-novartis/corporate-citizenship

Oxfam: www.oxfam.org

Pfizer Responsibility webpage: www.pfizer.com/responsibility

SustainAbility: www.sustainability.com

UNAIDS: www.unaids.org

SOCIETY AND ECONOMY

II

5

GLOBALISATION AND ITS CRITICS

Globalisation was supposed to break down barriers between continents and bring all peoples together. But what kind of globalisation do we have with over 1 billion people on the planet not having safe water to drink?

MIKHAIL GORBACHEV, former President of Russia

We have to act globally — not to overthrow globalisation, but to capture it for humanity's first democratic revolution.

GEORGE MONBIOT, British journalist and author

The essence of globalisation is a subordination of human rights, of labor rights, consumer rights, environmental rights, and democracy rights to the imperatives of global trade and investment.

RALPH NADER, American consumer activist and politician

In recent decades we have watched the free flow of ideas, individuals, investments and industries grow into an organic bond among developed economies. It is this borderless world that will give participating economies the capacity for boundless prosperity.

KENICHI OHMAE, author of *The Borderless World*

Questioning the benefits of economic globalisation...

The world has been globalising for thousands of years, steadily becoming more economically interconnected and interdependent due to advances in transport and communications technologies. However, it was Ricardo's economic theory of comparative advantage in 1800s that became the foundation for a movement — led by the world's richest countries — to liberalise (i.e. reduce barriers to) international trade.

The first wave of globalisation was led by the Victorian British Empire prior to World War I, but it wasn't until the 1944 Bretton Woods conference that the movement was institutionalised, including setting up the International Monetary Fund (IMF), World Bank and General Agreement on Tariffs and Trade (GATT).

In the decades that followed, debates about protectionism versus liberalisation continued to rage, but the free trade movement appeared to be steadily gaining ground. This was in no small measure due to the policy campaigns of annual leadership gatherings such as the World Economic Forum (in Davos, first convened in 1971) and the World Economic Summit (or so-called G7 Summit, first held in Rambouillet in 1975).

However, as the pro-globalisation, free trade movement coalesced around the GATT, signed in Marrakech in 1994 and superseded by the World Trade Organisation (WTO) the following year, so too did the anti-globalisation movement. The first cracks in the edifice of economic globali-

1944	Bretton Woods Conference held in New Hampshire
1971	First World Economic Forum (WEF) meeting held in Davos
1975	First World Economic (G7) Summit in Rambouillet
1994	General Agreement on Tariffs and Trade (GATT) signed in Marrakech
1995	World Trade Organisation (WTO) established
1998	Multilateral Agreement on Investment (MAI) abandoned
1999	WTO protests in Seattle
2001	First World Social Forum in Porto Alegre
2001	G8 Summit protests in Genoa
2005	Live 8 and Make Poverty History campaign

sation appeared when negotiations on the Multilateral Agreement on Investment (MAI) between members of the Organisation for Economic Cooperation and Development (OECD) were scrapped following a tidal wave of criticism by civil society organisations in 1997 and 1998.

Perhaps buoyed by the demise of the MAI, anti-globalisation protesters turned 1999 into a watershed year. Pressure began building, with protests at the EU Summit and G8 Summit in Cologne in June, and finally exploded at the WTO conference in Seattle in November. The 'Battle of Seattle', as the protests later became known, went down in history as the biggest demonstration in the US since civil rights and Vietnam protests. The WTO parties also failed to reach agreement on further negotiations.

Seattle set the precedent for anti-globalisation protests at subsequent multilateral meetings, including extremely violent clashes at the G8 Summit in Genoa in 2001. However, it also spawned more positive developments, such as the establishment of the World Social Forum, held annually in Porto Alegre since 2001, and the opening up of meetings such as the World Economic Forum to civil society participation.

Positive, peaceful mass demonstrations, such as Live 8 and the Make Poverty History campaign in 2005, also showed that globalisation issues — such as debt cancellation, aid and trade justice — are not just the concern of a fringe, anarchic minority. As a result, today, a smooth process of economic globalisation is no longer seen as an inevitable consequence of progress; and social and environmental concerns frequently rank at the top of international policy discussions and developments.

Protests against the G8 Summit in Heiligendamm, Germany
Randbild

Protests in Seattle and Genoa

The third World Trade Organisation (WTO) ministerial meeting was held in Seattle, USA, in December 1999. Talks collapsed after delegates failed to reach agreement on a new round of international trade agreements.

On the streets of Seattle, a wide range of protesters — opposed to WTO-style globalisation as a form of economic imperialism — battled for three days with riot police, at times bringing the WTO talks to a standstill. A state of civil emergency was declared. A curfew ran for two nights, and plastic bullets, tear gas, pepper spray, truncheons and water cannon were all used.

The 27th World Economic (or G8) Summit took place in Genoa, Italy, in July 2001. The overall theme of the summit was ways to reduce poverty, with topics including debt forgiveness to Heavily Indebted Poor Countries, the Global Health Fund, the global digital divide, the environment and food security.

There was a strong security presence amassed in preparation, and hundreds of thousands of demonstrators descended on the city, determined to highlight the G8's failure to deliver trade justice (e.g. through the elimination of agricultural subsidies in Europe and the USA) and inclusive globalisation. The Genoa protests turned into one of the most violent clashes in the history of the anti-globalisation movement, with hundreds of arrests and injuries, as well as one fatality.

FACTBOX

In Seattle:

- More than 100,000 marched on the conference.
- 500 people were arrested.
- Damages caused by the protesters were estimated at around $3 million.
- Business losses of more than $10 million were claimed.

In Genoa:

- 300,000 people took part in the protests.
- 20,000 police officers were deployed.
- 23-year-old Carlo Giuliani was fatally shot by a police officer during his attempt to attack a police van with a fire extinguisher.
- 231 people, including 121 demonstrators, 94 police officers and *carabinieri* as well as 16 journalists were injured, some of them seriously.
- Out of 93 people arrested during a police raid on a school being used as a dormitory by anti-globalisation demonstrators, 72 suffered injuries, and all were later released without charge.
- Some of the 288 arrested were retained in jail for weeks.
- Amnesty International (AI) claims that at least 200 protesters were tortured in Genoa.
- The physical damage from the protests was estimated at €50 million.
- In Italy, more than 10,000 people protested on July 24 against the actions of the police.

Anti-globalisation demonstrations in Seattle, USA, 1999

Reproduced with permission of Steve Kaiser

Live 8 and Make Poverty History

Make Poverty History — an alliance of 540 charities, trade unions and campaigning groups supported by leading public figures and celebrities — is a powerful example of the civil society movement challenging the world's most powerful institutions to make globalisation an inclusive process that the poorest nations can also benefit from.

In 2005, working in partnership with the Global Call to Action against Poverty, they used the G8 Summit in Gleneagles in July, and the corresponding Live 8 concerts, as a focal point for peaceful protests against poverty and injustice.

The campaign had three demands: (1) trade justice, including the end to perverse subsidies, (2) debt relief, including cancellation for the world's poorest countries, and (3) more and better aid, including $50 billion more in aid and a binding timetable for spending 0.7% of national income on aid.

With its high celebrity endorsement, linkage with the Live 8 concerts, clear demands, and simple symbol of a white wrist-band, the campaign was the largest and most successful campaign of its kind.

In addition to promises of extra aid, key policy outcomes included: (1) international acceptance of the principle of 100% multilateral debt cancellation for the poorest countries; (2) agreement that developing countries have the right to 'decide, plan and sequence their economic policies to fit with their own development strategies'; and (3) support for as close as possible to universal access to treatment for HIV and AIDS for all who need it by 2010.

FACTBOX

- ▶ The ten Live 8 concerts held on 2 July 2005, which made 'Make Poverty History' their central message, were said to have been watched by 3 billion people.
- ▶ 31 million people from 84 national coalitions around the world united in the Global Call to Action against Poverty, claiming to represent more than 150 million people in over 100 countries.
- ▶ 8 million people wore the Make Poverty History white wrist-band in the UK.
- ▶ On 2 July, over 225,000 people joined a peaceful march in Edinburgh to call on world leaders to act at the G8 summit in Gleneagles. Many of the campaigners were dressed in white to form the world's largest human white band around the city.

MAKEPOVERTY**HISTORY**

BOOKS

Joel Bakan, *The Corporation: The Pathological Pursuit of Profit and Power* (Free Press, 2005)

Charles Derber, *Corporation Nation: How Corporations Are Taking Over Our Lives and What We Can Do About It* (Saint Martin's Press, 1998)

Thomas Friedman, *The Lexus and the Olive Tree: Understanding Globalization* (Anchor, 2000)

Andrew Glynn, *Capitalism Unleashed: Finance, Globalization and Welfare* (Oxford University Press, 2006)

John Gray, *False Dawn: The Delusions of Global Capitalism* (Granta Books, 2002)

Stuart L. Hart, *Capitalism at the Crossroads: Aligning Business, Earth, and Humanity* (Wharton School Publishing, 2005)

Paul Hawken, *Blessed Unrest: How the Largest Movement in the World Came into Being and Why No One Saw It Coming* (Viking Press, 2007)

Hazel Henderson, *Beyond Globalization: Shaping a Sustainable Global Economy* (Kumarian Press, 1999)

Naomi Klein, *No Logo: No Space, No Choice, No Jobs* (Flamingo, 2002)

Naomi Klein, *The Shock Doctrine: The Rise of Disaster Capitalism* (Metropolitan Books, 2007)

David Korten, *When Corporations Rule the World* (Berrett-Koehler, 2001)

Jonathon Porritt, *Capitalism as If the World Matters* (Earthscan, 2005)

Leslie Sklair, *Globalization: Capitalism and Its Alternatives* (Oxford University Press, 3rd edn, 2002)

Joseph Stiglitz, *Globalization and Its Discontents* (W.W. Norton, 2002)

Joseph Stiglitz, *Making Globalization Work: The Next Steps to Global Justice* (Penguin Allen Lane, 2006)

Janet Thomas, *The Battle in Seattle: The Story Behind and Beyond the WTO Demonstrations* (Fulcrum Publishing, 2000)

WEBSITES

Attac: www.attac.org

WiserEarth: www.wiserearth.org

World Economic Forum: www.weforum.org

World Social Forum: www.wsf2008.net

World Trade Organisation (WTO): www.wto.org

WTO History Project: depts.washington.edu/wtohist/index.htm

on Mandela
essing the Make
erty History rally,
don, 2005
povertyhistory.org

6

POVERTY AND DEVELOPMENT

If we stop thinking of the poor as victims or as a burden and start recognizing them as resilient and creative entrepreneurs and value-conscious consumers, a whole new world of opportunity will open up.

C.K. PRAHALAD, Harvard Professor and author of *The Fortune at the Bottom of the Pyramid*

There is enough for everybody's need, but not for everybody's greed. Poverty is the worst form of violence.

MOHANDAS K. GANDHI

Overcoming poverty is not a gesture of charity. It is an act of justice. It is the protection of a fundamental human right, the right to dignity and a decent life.

NELSON MANDELA, former President of South Africa

Human development, as an approach, is concerned with what I take to be the basic development idea: namely, advancing the richness of human life, rather than the richness of the economy in which human beings live, which is only a part of it.

AMARTYA SEN, Professor of Economics, Harvard University, and Nobel Laureate in Economics (1998)

Closing the gap between 'haves' and 'have-nots'…

Tackling poverty and development has been a major international focus for at least the past 60 years, since the establishment of the International Bank for Reconstruction and Development in 1945. The initial approach of giving World Bank loans with conditional IMF structural adjustment programmes met with mixed success and growing resistance.

The efforts of development charities, on the other hand, such as those of CARE International (founded in 1946), World Vision (1950) and Christian Aid (1972), have been vital, but tend to address the symptoms rather than the cause of poverty. Even the landmark Live Aid event in 1985 provided only short-term solutions to the cyclical food insecurity and hunger crisis in Ethiopia at the time.

Meanwhile, the UN Development Programme, established in 1965, found poverty gaps between the richest and poorest increasing steadily year on year. In the 1980s, with the Third World debt crisis spiralling out of control, the approach began to change, with the multilateral institutions beginning to concede that export-led economic growth (as measured by GDP) may be an extremely limited, and often misleading, indicator of development.

The breakthrough came in 1990 when the UNDP introduced its Human Development Index (HDI), which is now calculated annually for 177 countries and measures national progress on three criteria: a long

1942	Oxfam (the Oxford Committee for Famine Relief) founded
1945	International Bank for Reconstruction and Development (IBRD) formed
1960	International Development Association (IDA) created
1965	United Nations Development Programme (UNDP) founded
1985	Live Aid concerts performed
1990	UN Human Development Index (HDI) launched
1997	UN Human Poverty Index (HPI) launched
2000	UN Millennium Development Goals (MDGs) launched
2002	'Bottom of the Pyramid' concept introduced by Hart and Prahalad
2005	Make Poverty History campaign and Live 8

and healthy life, knowledge (i.e. education) and a decent standard of living. The HDI has also been supplemented by two other measures: the Gender Related Development Index and Gender Empowerment Measure, both introduced in 1995, and Human Poverty Index, in 1997.

Another major shift occurred in 2000, when the UN adopted the Millennium Declaration, including eight measurable development goals to be achieved by 2015. These have served as a focal point for development efforts ever since, with considerable success in some countries, helped in no small measure by campaigns such as Live 8 and Make Poverty History in

2005 and the booming economies of China and India.

Until 2002, however, addressing these poverty and development issues was still seen very much as the responsibility of governments. This started to change when American professors Stuart Hart and C.K. Prahalad introduced the concept of the 'Bottom of the Pyramid', i.e. the business opportunities represented by the world's poorest 3 or 4 billion. Prahalad's 2004 book *The Fortune at the Bottom of the Pyramid* galvanised this new movement and sparked a lively debate on the role of business in poverty alleviation, which rages to this day.

Professor C.K. Prahalad
speaking at Interop,
Las Vegas, USA, 2008
© The Photo Group, 2008

Millennium Development Goals

The UN Millennium Development Goals (MDGs) are eight goals to be achieved by 2015 that respond to the world's main development challenges.

The MDGs are drawn from the actions and targets contained in the Millennium Declaration which was adopted by 189 nations and signed by 147 heads of state and governments during the UN Millennium Summit in September 2000.

The eight goals are:

Goal 1: Eradicate extreme poverty and hunger

Goal 2: Achieve universal primary education

Goal 3: Promote gender equality and empower women

Goal 4: Reduce child mortality

Goal 5: Improve maternal health

Goal 6: Combat HIV/AIDS, malaria and other diseases

Goal 7: Ensure environmental sustainability

Goal 8: Develop a Global Partnership for Development

In addition to the eight goals, there are 18 concrete targets measured using 48 indicators.

FACTBOX

- The proportion of people living in extreme poverty fell from nearly one-third to less than one-fifth between 1990 and 2004.
- If the trend is sustained, the MDG poverty reduction target will be met for the world as a whole and for most regions, except Africa and parts of the Middle East.
- However, the number of extremely poor people in sub-Saharan Africa has levelled off, and the poverty rate has declined by nearly six percentage points since 2000.
- Enrolment in primary education grew from 80% in 1991 to 88% in 2005.
- Child mortality has declined globally, malaria control has expanded, and the tuberculosis epidemic is on the verge of decline, although not fast enough to halve prevalence and death rates by 2015.
- Over half a million women still die each year from pregnancy and childbirth. The odds that a woman will die from these causes in sub-Saharan Africa are 1 in 16 over the course of her lifetime, compared to 1 in 3,800 in the developed world.
- According to the UN FAO, 14% of the world's population are undernourished. In sub-Saharan Africa, the figure is 31% and in South Asia 21%. If current trends continue, the target of halving the proportion of underweight children will be missed by 30 million children, largely because of slow progress in Southern Asia and sub-Saharan Africa.
- Half the population of the developing world lack basic sanitation. In order to meet the MDG target (which is related to MDG safe water drinking targets), an additional 1.6 billion people will need access to improved sanitation over the period 2005–15. If trends since 1990 continue, the world is likely to miss the target by almost 600 million people.

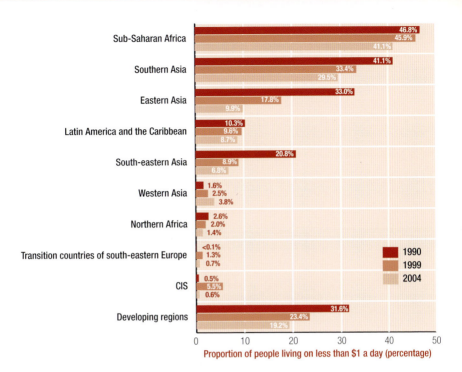

Figure 9 **Proportion of population in extreme poverty, by region (1990–2004)**
Source: *The Millennium Development Goals Report 2007* (New York: United Nations)

'Bottom of the Pyramid' markets

The Bottom (or Base) of the Pyramid (BOP) model refers both to the potential market of the 3–4 billion poorest people on Earth and private sector business models to address poverty.

This concept was introduced in a paper by Stuart Hart and C.K. Prahalad published in *Strategy + Business* in 2002 entitled 'The Fortune at the Bottom of the Pyramid' and expanded on in Prahalad's book of the same title in 2004.

The bottom of the pyramid refers to the 'survival economy', the group of people living on between $1 and $3 a day who can barely meet their basic needs, such as clean water, healthcare, education, housing and nutrition.

Due to their low incomes and perceived high risks, the BOP market has been largely underserved by traditional business. However, the BOP model suggests that there are enterprising ways to trade profitably in this market and alleviate poverty as a consequence.

The BOP model challenges conventional assumptions by suggesting that poor people are profitable, accessible, brand-conscious, highly connected and open to new technology.

The proposal of the BOP model is that business has to create the capacity to consume in three ways: through affordability, accessibility and availability.

BOP proponents argue that there is a need for new goods and services, but building trust in the communities is a prerequisite. When successful, BOP strategies restore dignity and choice to the poor.

The BOP model is not without its critics, however, who object to the Western consumerist approach and question the social and environmental impacts. They also question whether it results in multinationals simply undermining local businesses, and creating demand for products that are not needed.

FACTBOX

▶ According to Prahalad in 2004, nine countries — China, India, Brazil, Mexico, Russia, Indonesia, Turkey, South Africa and Thailand — have a combined GDP of $12.5 trillion (in Purchasing Power Parity terms), which represents 90% of the developing world. It is larger than the GDP of Japan, Germany, France, the United Kingdom and Italy combined.

▶ Cases often cited as successful examples of the BOP approach include: Aptech (India), Citibank Suvidha (India), Ericsson MiniGSM, Grameen Telecom (Bangladesh), Hindustan Lever (India), HP e-Inclusion, ITC (India), OphantIT.com (India/Philippines), Pioneer Hi-Bred (Latin America), PRODEM (Bolivia), TARAhaat (India), Voxia (Peru) and Women's Information Resource Electronic Service (Uganda).

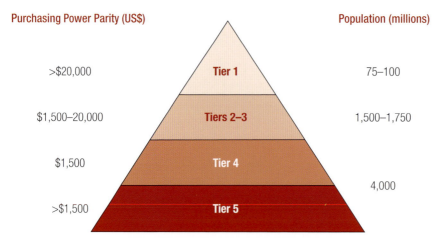

Figure 10 **The Bottom of the Pyramid model**

Source: C.K. Prahalad and Stuart Hart, 'The Fortune at the Bottom of the Pyramid', *Strategy+Business* 26 (2002). Reprinted with permission from *strategy+business*, published by Booz & Company. www.strategy-business.com.

BOOKS

Stuart L. Hart, *Capitalism at the Crossroads: Aligning Business, Earth and Humanity* (Wharton School Publishing, 2nd edn, 2005)

Michael Hopkins, *Corporate Social Responsibility and International Development: Is Business the Solution?* (Earthscan, 2006)

Manfred A. Max-Neef, *Human-Scale Development: Conception, Application and Further Reflections* (Zed Books, 1991)

C.K. Prahalad, *The Fortune at the Bottom of the Pyramid: Eradicating Poverty through Profits* (Wharton School Publishing, 2004)

Jeffrey D. Sachs, *The End of Poverty: Economic Possibilities for Our Time* (Penguin, 2005)

Amartya Sen, *Development as Freedom* (Oxford Paperbacks, new edn, 2000)

Vandana Shiva, *Staying Alive: Women, Ecology and Development* (Zed Books, 1989)

Muhammad Yunus, *Banker to the Poor: Micro-lending and the Battle against World Poverty* (Public Affairs, rev. edn, 2003)

REPORTS

Business and the Millennium Development Goals: A Framework for Action (International Business Leaders Forum [IBLF], 2005)

Business for Development: Business Solutions in Support of the Millennium Development Goals (World Business Council for Sustainable Development [WBCSD], 2005)

Doing Business with the Poor: A Field Guide (World Business Council for Sustainable Development [WBCSD], 2004)

Economic Multipliers: Revisiting the Core Responsibility and Contribution of Business to Development (Jane Nelson/International Business Leaders Forum [IBLF], 2003)

Exploring the Links between Wealth Creation and Poverty Reduction: A Case Study of Unilever in Indonesia (Oxfam and Unilever, 2005)

Human Development Report 2007/2008 (United Nations Development Programme [UNDP], 2008)

Measuring Unilever's Economic Footprint: The Case of South Africa (Ethan B. Kapstein/Unilever, 2008)

The Millennium Development Goals Report 2007 (United Nations)

The Next 4 Billion: Market Size and Business Strategy at the Base of the Pyramid (World Resources Institute [WRI], 2007)

WEBSITES

Base of the Pyramid Protocol: www.bop-protocol.org

CARE International: www.care.org

Christian Aid: www.christianaid.org

Human Development Reports: hdr.undp.org

International Business Leaders Forum (IBLF): www.iblf.org

MDG Monitor: www.mdgmonitor.org

Millennium Project: www.unmillenniumproject.org

NextBillion.net: www.nextbillion.net

Oxfam International: www.oxfam.org

UN Development Programme: www.undp.org

UN Millennium Development Goals: www.un.org/millenniumgoals

Unilever Environment and Society webpage: www.unilever.com/ourvalues/environment-society

World Business Council for Sustainable Development: www.wbcsd.org

World Vision: www.worldvision.org

7

HUMAN RIGHTS

Responsibility for the impact on human rights, both direct and indirect, is gaining ground. What have been seen as 'externalities' to company business are increasingly seen to need to be 'internalised', if companies are to succeed and survive in a more critical world.

SIR GEOFFREY CHANDLER, Founder Chair of Amnesty International UK Business Group

The UN Norms on Transnational Business set an important precedent in the struggle to make corporations accountable and liable for their actions everywhere and anywhere on this planet.

GREENPEACE

Campaigning and good business is also about putting forward solutions, not just opposing destructive practices or human rights abuses.

ANITA RODDICK, Founder and former CEO of The Body Shop International

Globalisation has contributed to impressive poverty reduction in major emerging market countries and overall welfare in the industrialised world. But it also imposes costs on people and communities — including corporate-related human rights abuses.

JOHN RUGGIE, UN Secretary-General's Special Representative on Human Rights, Transnational Corporations and Other Business Enterprises

Shackled by the ball and supply chain . . .

Although people have campaigned for human rights throughout history, it was only when the Universal Declaration of Human Rights was issued by the UN in 1948 that there was finally a common language and set of minimum standards against which to test allegations of abuse.

This was later supplemented by two other significant UN agreements on human rights: namely, the International Covenant on Economic, Social and Cultural Rights (in 1966) and the International Covenant on Civil and Political Rights (in 1976).

Seeing the need for an independent watchdog to ensure compliance with these standards, Amnesty International was set up in 1961 by British lawyer Peter Benenson as an activist organisation with the mission to uncover and publicise breaches of human rights and campaign to see them remedied.

It wasn't until the 1980s, especially after the Bhopal gas explosion, that human rights began to be discussed in a business context. For example, Amnesty still cites the 22,000 fatalities and 100,000 people who continue to suffer from chronic and debilitating illnesses caused by the gas leak as a case of human rights abuse by a company.

The issue once again hit the headlines in 1990s, most notably when Nigerian ac-

1948	Universal Declaration of Human Rights launched
1961	Amnesty International founded
1995	Nigerian government executes human rights activist Ken Saro-Wiwa
1997	TRAC Report accuses Nike of labour rights abuses in Vietnam
1997	SA8000 standard launched
1997	Fair Labor Association Workplace Code of Conduct launched
1998	International Labour Organisation (ILO) Declaration on Fundamental Principles and Rights at Work adopted
2000	Voluntary Principles on Security and Human Rights launched
2004	UN Norms on Business and Human Rights launched
2005	Business and Human Rights Resource Centre launched

tivist Ken Saro-Wiwa alleged Shell's complicity in human rights abuses of the Ogoni people and was executed by the Nigerian government in 1995. Around the same time, other oil and gas, mining, and forestry companies were coming under the spotlight for their negative impacts on indigenous tribes, with the likes of The Body Shop International mounting high-profile campaigns to raise awareness of their plight.

The emphasis of the debate shifted dramatically in 1997, when Nike was exposed for poor labour practices at one of its contract factories in Vietnam. Within months, there was a flood of allegations concerning human rights abuse in the supply chains of multinationals (with the term 'sweatshops' frequently being employed by critics and the media).

Among the positive initiatives to emerge from this period were several standards and codes addressing labour rights, including SA8000, the FLA (Fair Labor Association) Workplace Code of Conduct and the World Federation of Sporting Goods Industry Code of Conduct in 1997, as well as the ILO Declaration on Fundamental Principles and Rights at Work in 1988.

Beyond the narrow labour rights focus, more general standards were also developed, including the Voluntary Principles on Security and Human Rights in 2000 and the UN Norms on the Responsibilities of Transnational Corporations and Other Business Enterprises with Regard to Human Rights in 2004.

Subsequent efforts have focused on monitoring corporate compliance with these codes (by organisations such as Corp-Watch) and supporting companies that wish to proactively implement their prescriptions (through organisations such as the Business and Human Rights Resource Centre).

Nike labour rights exposé

In November 1997, the Transnational Resource and Action Center (TRAC, now called Corp-Watch), released a report called *Smoke from a Hired Gun: A Critique of Nike's Labor and Environmental Auditing in Vietnam as Performed by Ernst & Young*.

TRAC's report exposed the findings of a confidential January 1997 report for Nike by Ernst & Young (leaked by a disgruntled employee) entitled *Environmental and Labor Practice Audit of the Tae Kwang Vina Industrial Ltd Co., Vietnam*. The Ernst & Young document found various poor practices in areas of health and safety and working hours.

The *New York Times* picked up on the TRAC report which triggered a storm of negative publicity and pressure on Nike to address human rights in its supply chain.

Nike's initial response was to cite a report by Andrew Young of Good Works International (dated 27 June 1997), which evaluated Nike's Code of Conduct and its application at the factory level, concluding that 'Nike is doing a good job in the application of its Code of Conduct. But Nike can and should do better.' However, this just added to the controversy.

Among the more serious consequences was the *Nike v Kasky* case — a lawsuit filed in April 1998 in California against Nike for 'unlawful and unfair business practices' which violated California's Business and Professions Code. The lawsuit claimed that Nike made various misrepresentations about its standards of conduct.

Nike has since put a lot of effort and money into redressing its reputation, through a combination of public acknowledgements of past mistakes, stringent supply chain policies, factory audits, transparent reporting, and membership of partnerships such as the Global Alliance for Workers and Communities.

The industry has also responded with the World Federation of Sporting Goods Industry Code of Conduct, launched in 1997.

FACTBOX

▶ In 2006, Nike's three main product lines — footwear, apparel and equipment — used 800,000 workers in almost 700 contract factories in 52 countries.

▶ Today, Nike publishes a list of all contract factories currently approved to manufacture Nike-brand products, including those that are inactive.

▶ Between 2004 and 2006, Nike conducted 810 management audits in contract factories around the world, and in 2005 began collecting baseline environmental, health and safety data on more than 650 contract factories in 52 countries, conducting 65 audits and 15 in-depth root cause assessments.

▶ By 2011, Nike aims to eliminate excessive overtime and to run management training on workers' rights, women's rights, freedom of association and collective bargaining in its contract factories.

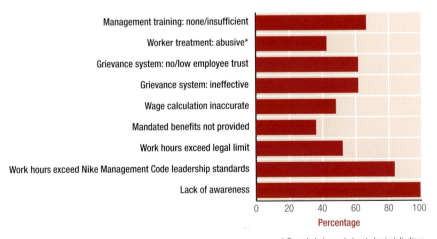

* Overwhelming verbal, not physical, findings

Figure 11 **Nike non-compliance management audit findings (2005/2006)**
Source: *Innovate for a Better World: Nike FY05–06 Corporate Responsibility Report*

UN Norms on Business and Human Rights

The UN Norms on the Responsibilities of Transnational Corporations and Other Business Enterprises with Regard to Human Rights ('the UN Norms') were put together by an expert body of the UN Sub-Commission on the Promotion and Protection of Human Rights and adopted in 2003.

The Norms set out a list of the human rights obligations of companies. They do not create new legal obligations, but simply explain how existing obligations under international law are relevant to companies and their global operations.

The Norms have not been universally accepted or embraced, with industry bodies such as the International Chamber of Commerce (ICC), International Organisation of Employers (IOE) and the US Council for International Business (USCIB), and governments such the US, arguing that enforcement of human rights is a state, not a private sector, responsibility.

FACTBOX

► The UN Norms contain substantive provisions on the following issues:
- Non-discrimination
- Protection of civilians and laws of war
- Use of security forces
- Workers' rights
- Corruption, consumer protection and human rights
- Economic, social and cultural rights
- Human rights and the environment
- Indigenous peoples' rights

► According to John Ruggie, in his report to the UN, of the more than 40 Alien Torts Claims Act cases brought against companies in the US, most have concerned alleged complicity, where the actual perpetrators were public or private security forces, other government agents, or armed factions in civil conflicts.

► The UN Human Rights Commission notes several actions being taken by progressive companies:
- Public acknowledgement of responsibility for human rights
- Institutionalising human rights within companies
- Board-level human rights oversight
- Human rights training
- Addressing indigenous persons
- Human rights impact assessments
- Innovative efforts to support core labour standards

NGOs such as Amnesty International, on the other hand, called for the Norms to be strengthened, and in 2005 the UN Human Rights Commission (HRC) issued a report on how this could be achieved. Harvard Professor John Ruggie was also appointed to the position of Special Representative, to identify and clarify existing issues related to business and human rights.

Today, many NGOs and some progressive companies (such as those in the Business Leaders Initiative on Human Rights) are using the UN Norms as a policy benchmark for improving their corporate responsibility performance.

Mary Robinson: 'In our Name' campaign

Oxfam

BOOKS

Karolien Bais and Mijnd Huijser, *The Profit of Peace: Corporate Responsibility in Conflict Regions* (Greenleaf Publishing, 2005)

Andrew Clapham, *Human Rights Obligations of Non-state Actors* (Oxford University Press, 2006)

Tim Connor, *Still Waiting for Nike to Do It: Nike's Labor Practices in the Three Years Since CEO Phil Knight's Speech to the National Press Club* (Global Exchange, 2001)

Radu Mares (ed.), *Business and Human Rights: A Compilation of Documents* (Brill, 2003)

Rory Sullivan (ed.), *Business and Human Rights: Dilemmas and Solutions* (Greenleaf Publishing, 2003)

REPORTS

Beyond Corporate Codes of Conduct: Work Organisation and Labour Standards at Nike's Suppliers (Richard Locke, Thomas Kochan, Monica Romis and Fei Qin in International Labour Review 146(1–2), pp. 21-40 [2007])

Business and Human Rights: A Geography of Corporate Risk (Amnesty International [UK] and International Business Leaders Forum [IBLF], 2002)

Business and Human Rights: A Progress Report (UN Human Rights Commission, 2000)

Business and Human Rights in a Time of Change (Christopher Avery, Amnesty International [UK], 2000)

Business and Human Rights: Mapping International Standards of Responsibility and Accountability for Corporate Acts (John Ruggie, 2007)

Embedding Human Rights in Business Practice (Global Compact and UN Human Rights Commission, 2004)

A Guide for Integrating Human Rights into Business Management (Business Leaders Initiative on Human Rights, 2007)

Human Rights: Is it Any of Your Business? (Amnesty International [UK] and International Business Leaders Forum [IBLF], 2000)

Human Rights: It is Your Business? The Case for Corporate Engagement (International Business Leaders Forum [IBLF], 2005)

Stabilization Clauses and Human Rights (International Finance Corporation [IFC] and UN Special Representative on Business and Human Rights, 2008)

WEBSITES

Amnesty International: www.amnesty.org

Business and Human Rights Resource Centre: www.business-humanrights.org

Business Leaders Initiative on Human Rights: www.blihr.org

CorpWatch: www.corpwatch.org

Fair Labor Association: www.fairlabor.org

ILO Declaration on Fundamental Principles and Rights at Work: www.ilo.org/declaration

Nike Responsibility webpage: nikeresponsibility.com

Social Accountability International: www.sa-intl.org

UN Human Rights: www.ohchr.org

Voluntary Principles on Security and Human Rights: www.voluntaryprinciples.org

World Federation of Sporting Goods Industry: www.wfsgi.org

8

CORRUPTION AND TRANSPARENCY

Criticism by rich countries of corruption in poor ones has little credibility while their financial institutions sit on wealth stolen from the world's poorest people.

AKERE MUNA, **Vice Chair of Transparency International**

Corruption is a major cause of poverty as well as a barrier to overcoming it... The two scourges feed off each other, locking their populations in a cycle of misery. Corruption must be vigorously addressed if aid is to make a real difference in freeing people from poverty.

PETER EIGEN, **Chairman, Extractive Industries Transparency Initiative**

Laws are going to be critical in reining in corruption. International charters can provide reformers both with an instrument with which to berate poor governance and a goal around which to unite.

DAVID COLLIER, **author of *The Bottom Billion***

Secrecy over state revenues encourages ruling elites to mismanage and misappropriate money rather than invest in long-term development.

GEORGE SOROS, **Chairman of the Open Society Institute**

'End Corruptio
Ugar
Reproduced with permis
of Kori

'Just say NC
Corruption', Zam
Lars Plough

Naming, shaming and setting principles...

The problem of bribery and corruption is nothing new. Indeed, Pliny the Elder is reputed to have said 'corruption of the best is worst' in around AD50. However, global efforts to highlight, measure and tackle corruption are comparatively new.

One of the most active and influential organisations has been Transparency International (TI), a global civil society organisation founded in 1993 with a mission to 'end the devastating impact of corruption on men, women and children around the world'. In 1995, TI launched its controversial Corruption Perceptions Index, ranking companies based on perceived public sector corruption.

The following year, the UN also adopted its Declaration Against Bribery and Corruption in Commercial Transactions, stating that this was necessary for an 'improved international business environment [to] enhance fairness and competitiveness'.

In 1999, the NGO Global Witness launched a campaign to put pressure on multinational corporations for the way in which they operate in countries that are in or emerging from conflict. Focusing on Angola, they issued a report entitled *A Crude Awakening: The Role of the Oil and Banking Industries in Angola's Civil War and the Plunder of State Assets*.

In 2001, BP became the first company to respond positively to the allegations of the report, stating that, in addition to maintaining a regular dialogue with both the World Bank and IMF over Angola, it would publish information annually on its operations in Angola. Sonangol (the Angolan state oil company) threatened to terminate BP's contract. However, in May 2004 the Angolan government announced that it would disclose some payments it receives from Western companies.

These commitments were broadened to encompass the whole sector, resulting in the development of the Extractive Industries Transparency Initiative, which was supported by the UK government and announced at the Johannesburg Summit in 2002. In the same year, the Publish What You Pay Campaign was launched by financier George Soros, and TI and Social Accountability International launched the Business Principles for Countering Bribery, providing a generic code for companies seeking to adopt a comprehensive anti-bribery programme.

As momentum gathered, 2003 saw the adoption of the UN Convention Against Corruption and the launch of TI's Global Corruption Barometer, with the addition to the UN Global Compact of a 10th principle, on anti-corruption, in 2004. This was essential, as then Secretary-General Kofi Annan put it, to 'address one of the most pernicious obstacles to growth and development'.

Today, bribery and corruption is increasingly recognised as a global problem, with Western multinationals being as complicit as developing-country governments. For this reason, TI launched its Bribe Payers' Index in 2006 to monitor export countries that are more inclined to pay bribes to do business in emerging-market host countries.

1993	Transparency International founded
1995	Transparency International's Corruption Perceptions Index (CPI) released
1996	UN Declaration Against Bribery and Corruption adopted
2002	Business Principles for Countering Bribery launched
2002	Publish What You Pay campaign launched
2003	Extractive Industries Transparency Initiative (EITI) launched
2003	UN Convention Against Corruption adopted
2003	Transparency International's Global Corruption Barometer launched
2004	Anti-corruption added as 10th principle of UN Global Compact
2006	Transparency International's Bribe Payers' Index launched

Transparency International indexes

Transparency International, founded in 1993, and now active in more than 90 countries, has three main indexes: the Corruption Perceptions Index, Bribe Payers' Index and Global Corruption Barometer.

The annual Corruption Perceptions Index, first released in 1995, ranks more than 180 countries in terms of perceived levels of public sector corruption. It is a composite index that draws on 14 expert opinion surveys.

The Bribe Payers' Index assesses the supply side of corruption and ranks corruption in 15 emerging-market countries and 17 industry sectors.

The Global Corruption Barometer is a public opinion survey that assesses the general public's perception and experience of corruption in more than 60 countries around the world.

Transparency International's recommendations include:

- Improved enforcement of the OECD Anti-Bribery Convention
- Voluntary adoption of the Convention by China, India and Russia

- Debarment by multilateral development banks of companies found guilty of foreign bribery
- Corruption due diligence investigations by companies when engaging in partnerships or acquisitions
- Adoption and enforcement of strict internal no-bribes corporate policies that include their agents, subsidiaries and branches
- Prosecution of foreign companies found to have bribed in developing countries

FACTBOX

According to the 2007 Corruption Perceptions Index:

▶ 40% of countries where corruption is perceived as rampant are classified by the World Bank as low-income countries.

▶ Public sector corruption is perceived as lowest in New Zealand, Denmark and Finland, and highest in Myanmar, Somalia and Iraq.

According to the 2007 Global Corruption Barometer:

▶ About 1 in 10 people around the world had to pay a bribe in the past year.

▶ Reported bribery has increased in some regions, such as Asia-Pacific and South East Europe.

▶ The general public believes political parties, parliament, the police and the judicial/legal system are the most corrupt institutions in their societies.

▶ Half of those interviewed — and significantly more than four years ago — expect corruption in their country to increase in the next three years, with some African countries being the exception.

▶ Half of those interviewed also think that their government's efforts to fight corruption are ineffective.

According to the 2006 Bribe Payers' Index:

▶ The export countries perceived as most likely to pay bribes in emerging-market economies are India, China, Russia, Turkey and Taiwan, while those least likely to pay bribes are Switzerland, Sweden, Australia, Austria and Canada.

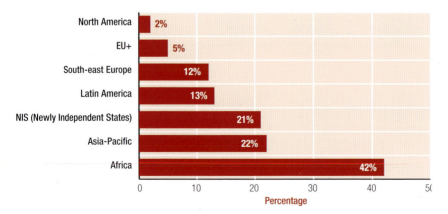

Figure 12 **Percentage of respondents who paid a bribe to obtain services (by region)**

Source: *Report on the Transparency International Global Corruption Barometer 2007*

'Please do not corrupt us', Freetown Airport, Sierra Leone

Reproduced with permission of Robert Rogoyski

Extractive Industries Transparency Initiative (EITI)

The Extractive Industries Transparency Initiative (EITI) is a coalition of governments, companies, civil society groups, investors and international organisations. It was announced by UK Prime Minister Tony Blair at the Johannesburg Summit in 2002 and was launched in 2003.

The EITI aims to strengthen governance by improving transparency and accountability in the extractives sector. It does this by supporting full publication and verification of company payments and government revenues from oil, gas and mining in resource-rich countries.

The EITI is founded on the following principles:

- Natural resources wealth should lead to growth and poverty reduction
- Transparency is essential in order to achieve this
- All parties must be involved in the process of creating transparency
- The process to create transparency should always respect the sovereignty of countries and existing contracts and laws

In 2008, 15 countries were considered Candidate Countries and can proceed to implementation. These countries have two years to establish themselves as fully compliant and include: Azerbaijan, Cameroon, Gabon, Ghana, Guinea, Kazakhstan, Kyrgyzstan, Liberia, Mali, Mauritania, Mongolia, Niger, Nigeria, Peru and Yemen. Seven of these have already published audited reports.

For a further nine countries, additional information is required before a decision about candidate status can be considered. These include: Chad, Democratic Republic of Congo, Equatorial Guinea, Madagascar, Republic of Congo, São Tomé and Principe, Sierra Leone, Trinidad & Tobago and Timor-Leste.

In 2008, the World Bank launched its own initiative (EITI++), with the support of the EITI, to extend transparency in this sector beyond revenues. The Bank plans to provide governments with technical assistance and capacity building to improve the management of resource-related wealth for the benefit of the poor.

FACTBOX

▶ 3.5 billion people live in countries rich in oil, gas and minerals. According to EITI, with good governance the exploitation of these resources can generate large revenues to foster growth and reduce poverty. However, when governance is weak, it may result in poverty, corruption and conflict.

▶ In a 2006 review of progress since the launch of EITI four years earlier, Publish What You Pay and Revenue Watch Institute found that:

- Twenty-one governments of resource-rich countries in Africa, Asia, Latin America and Central Asia have endorsed the initiative
- The International Advisory Group (IAG) has developed many of the necessary guidelines, criteria and governance structures
- Two countries have published fully audited and reconciled EITI reports
- Eight countries have yet to take the initial step of appointing an individual to lead the EITI process
- Ten countries have not yet formed the required multi-stakeholder committee
- Eleven countries do not have a drafted and approved work plan

EITI visit to Newmont Mine in Ghana
Reproduced with permission of EITI Secretariat

BOOKS

Transparency International, *The TI Source Book 2000: Confronting Corruption: The Elements of a National Integrity System* (Transparency International, 2000)

Transparency International, *Corruption Fighters' Tool Kit: Teaching Integrity to Youth: Examples from 11 Countries* (Transparency International, 2004)

Transparency International, *The TI Anti-corruption Handbook (ACH): National Integrity System in Practice* (Transparency International, 2007)

REPORTS

Business Principles for Countering Bribery (Transparency International and Social Accountability, 2002)

Bribe Payers' Index (Transparency International, 2006)

Corruption Perceptions Index (Transparency International, 2007)

A Crude Awakening: The Role of the Oil and Banking Industries in Angola's Civil War and the Plunder of State Assets (Global Witness, 1999)

Eye on EITI: Civil Society Perspectives and Recommendations on the Extractive Industries (Transparency Initiative, Publish What You Pay and Revenue Watch Institute, 2006)

Global Corruption Barometer (Transparency International, 2007)

Global Corruption Report 2007 (Transparency International, 2007)

UN Convention Against Corruption (United Nations, 2003)

UN Declaration Against Bribery and Corruption (United Nations, 1996)

WEBSITES

Extractive Industries Transparency Initiative: eitransparency.org

Global Witness: www.globalwitness.org

Internet Center for Corruption Research: www.icgg.org

Publish What You Pay: www.publishwhatyoupay.org

Revenue Watch Institute: www.revenuewatch.org

Transparency International: www.transparency.org

UN Global Compact: www.globalcompact.org

B

GLOBAL RESPONSES

THE UNIVERSAL DECLARATION OF Human Rights

III

LEADERSHIP

9

WORLD SUMMITS

The Earth Summit is not an end in itself but a new beginning. The road beyond Rio will be a long and difficult one; but it will also be a journey of renewed hope, of excitement, challenge and opportunity, leading as we move into the 21st century to the dawning of a new world in which the hopes and aspirations of all the world's children for a more secure and hospitable future can be fulfilled.

MAURICE STRONG, Secretary-General of the Rio Earth Summit

Rio was a grand vision, a road map. But a road map is not quite enough for starting to travel. You also need a route plan. You need to say I am going to start here and end there, and these are the resources I am going to use.

NITIN DESAI, Secretary-General of the Johannesburg World Summit on Sustainable Development

The [Johannesburg] Summit represents a major leap forward in the development of partnerships, with the UN, governments, business and civil society coming together to increase the pool of resources to tackle global problems on a global scale. We have to go out and take action.

KOFI ANNAN, former Secretary-General of the UN

The peoples of the world expect that this World Summit will live up to its promise of being a fitting culmination to a decade of hope, by adopting a practical programme for the translation of the dream of sustainable development into reality and bringing into being a new global society that is caring and humane.

THABO MBEKI, former President of South Africa

WSSD Sur
Secretary-Ger
Nitin Desai spea
at the first ple
session, August 2
UN

Negotiating our way around the global commons...

The convening of world governments to address global challenges is part of the mandate of the United Nations. However, the past 20 years witnessed an astounding growth in scale and ambition of these UN meetings, reflecting not only the trend towards globalisation but also the increasing severity of the problems facing the world, and the urgency to find international solutions.

After its first world conference to focus on the environment — held in Stockholm in 1972 — and another in Vancouver in 1978 addressing development issues, the UN saw the need to bring these two areas together. Hence, the World Commission on Environment and Development was established in 1983, under the chairmanship of Gro Harlem Brundtland, Prime Minister of Norway.

The work of the Commission, summarised in its 1987 report *Our Common Future* (commonly known as the Brundtland Report), had a profound effect on global policy development, not least because of its cleverly crafted concept of 'sustainable development', which seemed an acceptable compromise between the economic growth ambitions of the 'North', the human development needs of the 'South' and the physical limitations of the Earth.

The Brundtland Report led directly to the 'Earth Summit', held in Rio de Janeiro in

1964	UN Conference on Trade and Development in Geneva
1972	UN Conference on the Human Environment in Stockholm
1978	UN Conference on Human Settlements (Habitat I) in Vancouver
1992	UN Conference on Environment and Development (the 'Earth Summit') in Rio de Janeiro
1993	UN World Conference on Human Rights in Vienna
1994	UN International Conference on Population and Development in Cairo
1995	World Summit for Social Development in Copenhagen
1996	World Food Summit in Rome
2000	UN Millennium Summit in New York
2002	UN World Summit on Sustainable Development in Johannesburg

1992 — the biggest international meeting of heads of state in history. Although criticised for the marginal involvement it allowed civil society and business, as well as for its overly 'green' focus and neglect of pressing social issues, the Summit's outputs — including its Agenda 21 programme and climate change and biodiversity conventions — have focused huge global efforts on tackling these issues.

So began the decade of UN 'mega-summits', which included world conferences on human rights (Vienna, 1993), population and development (Cairo, 1994), social development (Copenhagen, 1995), women (Beijing, 1995), human settlements (Habitat II, Istanbul, 1996), food (Rome, 1996), sustainable development (Rio+5, New York, 1997) and development (Millennium Summit, New York, 2000).

In parallel, the institutions set up at Rio were also convening major international meetings. For example, the first Conference of the Parties (COP-1) of the UN Framework Convention on Climate Change (UNFCCC) met in Berlin in 1995 and annually thereafter, concluding the historic Kyoto Protocol at COP-3 in Japan in 1997.

Ten years after the Rio Summit, the World Summit on Sustainable Development in Johannesburg was held in 2002 to review progress. With a growing sense of the failure of the mega-summits to deliver on their promises, much of the emphasis at the Summit was on practical actions and cross-sector partnerships to deliver sustainable development.

Subsequent gatherings have been smaller in scale and more focused on specific issues — such as monitoring implementation of the Millennium Development Goals — and tangible outcomes — such as an inclusive post-Kyoto international agreement, which was widely called for at the UN Climate Change Conference in Bali in 1997.

Rio Earth Summit

The United Nations Conference on Environment and Development (UNCED), popularly known as the 'Earth Summit', was held in Rio de Janeiro from 3–14 June 1992.

The Summit was chaired by Canadian business and development leader Maurice F. Strong, who was also Secretary-General of the 1972 United Nations Conference on the Human Environment in Stockholm.

The principal themes of the conference were environment and sustainable development, the latter having been coined in the 1987 Brundtland Report (entitled *Our Common Future*), issued by the World Commission on Environment and Development, which Norwegian Prime Minister Gro Harlem Brundtland had chaired since 1983.

The now classic Brundtland definition of sustainable development, which the Summit helped to popularise and embed, is 'development that meets the needs of the present without compromising the ability of future generations to meet their own needs'.

FACTBOX

- ▶ 172 governments participated in the Summit, 108 at the level of heads of state or government, making this the biggest and most senior world conference ever organised.
- ▶ The UN claims 47,000 people converged on Rio to be part of the Summit and its associated activities.
- ▶ 2,400 representatives of NGOs were officially included in the Summit, and 17,000 people attended the parallel Global Forum.
- ▶ The Summit was covered by 10,000 on-site journalists.
- ▶ The Summit cost the UN $10 million to organise.
- ▶ In addition to the 108 countries that adopted Agenda 21, over 1,800 cities and towns worldwide have since created their own Local Agenda 21.

Outputs of the Summit included three major agreements:

- Agenda 21: a comprehensive programme (of 900 pages in 4 sections and 40 chapters) for global action in all areas of sustainable development

- The Rio Declaration on Environment and Development: a series of 27 principles defining the rights and responsibilities of States

- The Statement of Forest Principles: a set of principles to underlie the sustainable management of forests worldwide

The Summit also adopted two binding conventions:

- The United Nations Framework Convention on Climate Change

- The Convention on Biological Diversity

The United Nations Convention to Combat Desertification, adopted in 1994, also resulted directly from the Summit.

The main follow-up mechanism is the Commission on Sustainable Development, which meets annually in New York to review progress. It focuses on a particular theme in two-year cycles.

Johannesburg World Summit

The UN World Summit on Sustainable Development (WSSD) — also known as the Earth Summit +10 or the Johannesburg Summit — was held from 26 August to 4 September 2002 in South Africa. The main objective was to focus on the implementation of Agenda 21. It was the biggest international gathering ever held in Africa.

There were three major outputs from the Summit:

- The Johannesburg Declaration on Sustainable Development: where heads of state and government committed to taking the action needed to make sustainable development a reality

- The Johannesburg Plan of Implementation: negotiated by governments, which sets out in more detail the action needed in specific areas

- Partnerships: including commitments by governments and other stakeholders to a broad range of partnership activities and initiatives that would implement sustainable development at the national, regional and international levels

The 'Greening the WSSD' Initiative was established to ensure that the Summit was organised along environmental best-practice lines and that minimal waste was generated by the thousands of delegates that descended on Johannesburg.

FACTBOX

- 191 countries attended the Summit, including 100 heads of state and government. There were around 22,000 participants, including 10,000 delegates accredited by the UN to attend the Summit. In addition, some 8,000 representatives of major stakeholder group organisations and 4,000 media were accredited to the Summit.

- Over 2,000 representatives of businesses and business organisations participated in the Summit and parallel events in Johannesburg, half of which were international. Business groups estimate that 700 companies were represented and between 40 and 50 CEOs participated.

- An NGO event also took place in parallel, with over 500 civil society organisations taking part, leading to the development of the Global People's Forum Civil Society Declaration.

- Over 220 partnerships (with $235 million in resources) were identified in advance of the Summit and around 60 partnerships were announced during the Summit, including major initiatives by the US, Japan, UK, Germany, France and the EU.

- Notwithstanding severe international and *in situ* criticism of the absence of President Bush at the Summit and the obstructive policy position of the US on climate change, the US announced five initiatives: tackling water for the poor ($970 million), clean energy ($43 million), hunger in Africa ($90 million) and HIV/AIDS, tuberculosis and malaria ($1.2 billion).

BOOKS

Kenny Bruno and Joshua Karliner, *Earthsummit.Biz: The Corporate Takeover of Sustainable Development* (Food First, 2003)

Minu Hemmati with Felix Dodds, Jasmin Enayati and Jan McHarry, *Multi-stakeholder Processes for Governance and Sustainability* (Earthscan, 2002)

Luc Hens and Bhaskar Nath, *The World Summit on Sustainable Development: The Johannesburg Conference* (Springer, 2005)

Chad Holliday, Stephan Schmidheiny and Philip Watts, *Walking The Talk: The Business Case for Sustainable Development* (Greenleaf Publishing, 2002)

Jan McHarry, Janet Strachan, Rosalie Callway and Georgina Ayre, *The Plain Language Guide to the World Summit on Sustainable Development* (Earthscan, 2004)

Stephan Schmidheiny with the World Business Council for Sustainable Development (WBCSD)*, Changing Course: A Global Business Perspective on Development and the Environment* (MIT Press, 1992)

Daniel Sitarz (ed.), *Agenda 21: The Earth Summit Strategy to Save Our Planet* (Earth Press, 1993)

United Nations Environment Programme, *Negotiating and Implementing Multilateral Environmental Agreements (MEAs): A Manual for NGOs* (UNEP/Earthprint, 2007)

REPORTS

Agenda 21 (UN, 1992)

The Johannesburg Declaration on Sustainable Development (UN, 2002)

The Johannesburg Plan of Implementation (UN, 2002)

The Millennium Declaration (UN, 2000)

The Rio Declaration on Environment and Development (UN, 1992)

Signals of Change: Business Progress towards Sustainable Development (World Business Council for Sustainable Development [WBCSD], 1997)

WEBSITES

Agenda 21: www.un.org/esa/sustdev/documents/agenda21/english/agenda21toc

Earth Summit 2002: www.earthsummit2002.org

Earth Summit Info: www.earthsummit.info

IIED (International Institute for Sustainable Development) WSSD Portal: www.iisd.ca/wssd/portal.html

Stakeholder Forum for a Sustainable Future: www.stakeholderforum.org

UN Conferences and Summits webpage: www.un.org/esa/devagenda

UN Rio Earth Summit: www.un.org/geninfo/bp/enviro

UN Earth Summit +5: www.un.org/esa/earthsummit

UN International Conference on Population and Development: www.unfpa.org/icpd

UN Millennium Summit: www.un.org/millennium

UN World Conference on Human Rights: www.unhchr.ch/html/menu5/wchr.htm

UN Johannesburg World Summit: www.un.org/jsummit/html/basic_info/basicinfo

UN Sustainable Development webpage: www.un.org/esa/sustdev

UN World Summit on Social Development: www.un.org/esa/socdev/wssd

World Summit 2002: www.worldsummit2002.org

ning ceremony of
WSSD,
annesburg, South
ca, August 2004
hoto

10
BUSINESS ASSOCIATIONS

Over the last 25 years, we have learned that responsible business practice builds competitive businesses and cohesive and sustainable societies. So we now need to learn from different experiences and we also need innovation: we need a new determination to raise the game.

HRH THE PRINCE OF WALES, President, Business in the Community

We need business to give practical meaning and reach to the values and principles that connect cultures and people everywhere.

BAN KI-MOON, UN Secretary-General

I am proud to be playing a part in a body that has helped businesses to work together to champion responsible business ... at a time when every business needs to address the major environmental, ethical and social challenges facing our world — challenges which are too large for any one organisation to address alone.

SIR STUART ROSE, Chief Executive, Marks & Spencer, and Chairman, Business in the Community

Business cannot succeed in societies that fail.

BJÖRN STIGSON, President of the World Business Council for Sustainable Development (WBCSD)

Kofi Annan address
the Global Comp
Leaders Summit, N
York, 20
UN P

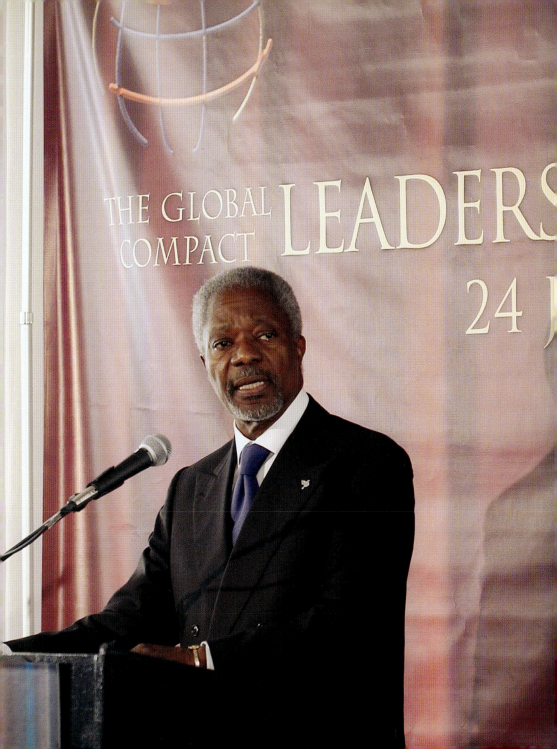

The drive for voluntary self-regulation...

The formation of global or regional business associations as a route to collective representation, influence and action is nothing new. Indeed, the International Chamber of Commerce (ICC) was established as long ago as 1919. However, business associations dedicated to positive action on issues of sustainability and responsibility are a more recent phenomenon.

One of the earliest examples is Ashoka, a global association of 1,800 social entrepreneurs in 60 countries, which was established in 1980 to link together 'men and women with system changing solutions for the world's most urgent social problems'. Others are Business in the Community and the International Business Leaders Forum, founded in 1982 and 1990 respectively under the presidency of HRH the Prince of Wales as a corporate response to significant social and environmental problems in the UK and around the world.

Ten years later, the Rio Earth Summit served as a catalyst for a more global business response to the challenges of sustainable development. First, the ICC prepared a 16-principle Business Charter for Sustainable Development, which has subsequently been signed by thousands of companies in 130 countries. Second, Swiss industrialist Stephan Schmidheiny set up the Business Council for Sustainable Development (BCSD) as Principal

1980	Ashoka social enterprise network founded in the USA
1982	Business in the Community founded in the UK
1990	International Business Leaders Forum (IBLF) founded in the UK
1992	Business for Social Responsibility (BSR) founded in the USA
1995	World Business Council for Sustainable Development (WBCSD) created
1997	Social Venture Network founded in Europe
1997	Forum Empresa (responsible business network) in Latin America founded
2000	UN Global Compact launched
2001	African Institute for Corporate Citizenship (AICC) founded
2004	CSR Asia founded

Advisor for Business and Industry to Maurice Strong, Secretary-General of the Earth Summit.

The BCSD led, in 1995, to the establishment of the World Business Council for Sustainable Development (WBCSD) after a merger with the World Industry Council on the Environment. Then, in 2000, Secretary-General Kofi Annan launched the UN Global Compact as a way to 'catalyse business actions in support of broader UN goals', inviting companies to commit themselves to ten principles on human rights, labour, environment and corruption.

In addition to these global initiatives, regional business networks have also flourished, including CSR Europe (established in 1995), Forum Empresa (1997), the African Institute for Corporate Citizenship (2001) and CSR Asia (2004). Likewise, national business associations have added to the momentum, with organisations such as Business in the Community (founded in 1982), Business for Social Responsibility in the USA (1992) and the National Business Initiative in South Africa (1995), to name but a few.

As a general rule, these business associations tend to favour voluntary self-regulation and market-based approaches to advancing sustainability, relying on the 'business case' to incentivise action. Critics argue that, at its worst, this leads to lobbying against policy reforms that would favour sustainability, and, at best, incremental change geared to maintaining the status quo, rather than the sort of transformational change needed to address global sustainability challenges.

Despite these criticisms, there are contrary examples, such as the Prince of Wales's Corporate Leaders Group on Climate Change, which 'believe that there is an urgent need to develop new and longer-term policies for tackling climate change'. Hence, they, together with others such as the US Climate Action Partnership, are lobbying for more, rather than less, regulation, in order to have a predictable policy framework and investment horizon.

World Business Council for Sustainable Development (WBCSD)

The World Business Council for Sustainable Development (WBCSD) is a CEO-led global association of companies dealing exclusively with business and sustainable development.

The WBCSD was created in 1995 from a merger between the Business Council for Sustainable Development (BCSD), founded in 1992 on the eve of the Rio Earth Summit by Swiss industrialist Stephan Schmidheiny, and the World Industry Council on the Environment.

The 200 member companies are drawn from more than 35 countries and 20 major industrial sectors. The Council also benefits from a global network of about 55 national and regional business councils and regional partners.

The Council provides a platform for companies to explore sustainable development, share knowledge, experiences and best practices, and to advocate business positions on these issues in a variety of forums, working with governments, non-governmental and intergovernmental organisations.

The Council focuses on four key areas: (1) energy and climate, (2) development, (3) the business role, and (4) ecosystems.

Current projects include: Energy Efficiency in Buildings, Water and Sustainable Development, Capacity Building, and the Eco-patent Commons.

Industry initiatives include: the Cement Sustainability Initiative, Electricity Utilities, Sustainable Forest Products Industry, Mining, Minerals and Sustainable Development, Sustainable Mobility, and the Tyre Industry.

In 2007, the Council published 27 major documents, had extensive press coverage, and, according to technorati.com, the Council was mentioned in more than 1,000 blogs. The WBCSD's website had a record 1.5 million visitors last year accessing some 4 million pages.

FACTBOX

▶ WBCSD has distilled its philosophy and experience into ten key messages:

1. Business is good for sustainable development and sustainable development is good for business
2. Business cannot succeed in societies that fail
3. Poverty is a key enemy to stable societies
4. Access to markets for all supports sustainable development
5. Good governance is needed to make business a part of the solution
6. Business has to earn its licence to operate, innovate and grow
7. Innovation and technology development are crucial to sustainable development
8. Eco-efficiency — doing more with less — is at the core of the business case for sustainable development
9. Ecosystems in balance is a prerequisite for business
10. Cooperation beats confrontation

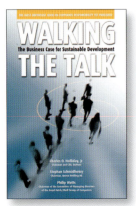

Publications of the World Business Council for Sustainable Development
WBCSD

UN Global Compact

Launched by the (then) UN Secretary-General Kofi Annan in 2000, the UN Global Compact is a framework for businesses that are committed to aligning their operations and strategies with ten universally accepted principles in the areas of human rights, labour, the environment and anti-corruption.

The Compact is the world's largest global corporate responsibility initiative, with over 5,000 participants, including over 3,600 businesses in 100 countries.

The Compact is a purely voluntary initiative with two objectives: (1) mainstream the ten principles in business activities around the world; and (2) catalyse actions in support of broader UN goals, such as the Millennium Development Goals (MDGs).

A company that signs up to the Compact specifically commits itself to: (1) set in motion changes to business operations so that the Global Compact and its principles become part of management, strategy, culture and day-to-day operations; (2) publish in its annual report or similar public corporate report (e.g. sustainability report) a description of the ways in which it is supporting the Global Compact and its principles; and (3) publicly advocate the Global Compact and its principles via communications vehicles such as press releases and speeches.

The voluntary, self-declaration approach of the Compact has led to widespread criticism that it lacks substance and sanction. As one critic put it in an UNRISD paper, "The Global Compact does more to enhance the image and legitimacy of big business than to improve social and environmental standards.'

As a result, the Compact has become more vigilant about monitoring participating companies, with over 900 companies marked as 'inactive' or delisted in January 2008.

Ban Ki-moon addresses the opening of the Global Compact Leaders Summit, Geneva, 2007
UN Photo

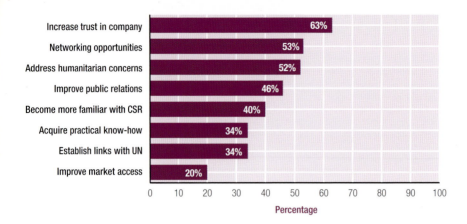

Figure 13 **What are the reasons for your organisation's participation in the Global Compact?**

Source: *UN Global Compact Annual Review: 2007 Leaders Summit* (New York: Global Compact)

FACTBOX

The UN Global Compact's ten principles are:

Human rights

1. Businesses should support and respect the protection of internationally proclaimed human rights; and
2. Make sure that they are not complicit in human rights abuses.

Labour standards

3. Businesses should uphold the freedom of association and the effective recognition of the right to collective bargaining;
4. The elimination of all forms of forced and compulsory labour;
5. The effective abolition of child labour; and
6. The elimination of discrimination in respect of employment and occupation.

Environment

7. Businesses should support a precautionary approach to environmental challenges;
8. Undertake initiatives to promote greater environmental responsibility; and
9. Encourage the development and diffusion of environmentally friendly technologies.

Anti-corruption

10. Businesses should work against corruption in all its forms, including extortion and bribery.

BOOKS

Claude Fussler, Aron Cramer and Sebastian van der Vegt, *Raising the Bar: Creating Value with the UN Global Compact* (Greenleaf Publishing, 2004)

Chad Holliday, Stephan Schmidheiny and Philip Watts, *Walking The Talk: The Business Case for Sustainable Development* (Greenleaf Publishing, 2002)

Malcolm McIntosh, Sandra Waddock and Georg Kell (eds.), *Learning to Talk: Corporate Citizenship and the Development of the UN Global Compact* (Greenleaf Publishing, 2004)

Stephan Schmidheiny with the World Business Council for Sustainable Development (WBCSD), *Changing Course: A Global Business Perspective on Development and the Environment* (MIT Press, 1992)

Sandrine Tesner and Georg Kell, *The United Nations and Business: A Partnership Recovered* (Palgrave Macmillan, 2000)

REPORTS

For a full list of downloadable WBCSD publications and reports, see www.wbcsd.org. Recent reports include:

Doing Business with the World: The New Role of Corporate Leadership in Global Development

Establishing a Global Carbon Market

Investing in a Low-Carbon Energy Future in the Developing World

Markets for Ecosystem Services: New Challenges and Opportunities for Business and the Environment

Powering a Sustainable Future: Policies and Measures to Make it Happen

For a full list of downloadable UN Global Compact publications and reports, see www.unglobalcompact.org. Recent reports include:

Business Fighting Corruption: Experiences from Africa

Business Guide to Partnering with NGOs and the United Nations

Caring for Climate: Tomorrow's Leadership Today

The CEO Water Mandate

Guide to Human Rights Impact Assessment and Management

WEBSITES

African Institute of Corporate Citizenship: www.aiccafrica.org

Ashoka: ashoka.org

Business for Social Responsibility: www.bsr.org

Business in the Community: www.bitc.org.uk

CSR Asia: www.csr-asia.com

CSR Europe: www.csreurope.org

CSR International: www.csrinternational.org

Forum Empresa: www.empresa.org

Social Venture Network: www.svn.org

UN Global Compact: www.unglobalcompact.org

World Business Council for Sustainable Development: www.wbcsd.org

11
LEADERSHIP INITIATIVES

Globalisation is forcing changes in how people collaborate in a fundamental way. You need stronger and stronger collaborative political leadership. If we are interconnected and the world is interconnected, the only way for the world to work is to have a set of common values. We have no option but to work together.

TONY BLAIR, former UK Prime Minister

We are convinced that the future of humankind is not determined once and for all and that each human being can contribute to the improvement of our societies.

CLUB OF ROME

The turmoil in the financial markets . . . [has] shown us that the globalization process needs to take much more into account the social dimension and the real interests of people.

KLAUS SCHWAB, Founder and President of the World Economic Forum

We are millions of women and men, organisations, networks, movements, trade unions from all parts of the world, we come from villages, regions, rural zones, urban centres, we are of all ages, peoples, cultures, beliefs, but we are united by the strong conviction that another world is possible!

WORLD SOCIAL FORUM

'Call to Action o
Millen
Development G
during the
Annual Meeting o
World Econo
Forum in Da
Switzerl
25 January
World Economic

With greater power comes greater responsibility . . .

There have always been individual leaders who have taken a stand on social and environmental issues. However, as political and economic globalisation has increased, several platforms have emerged where international leaders deliberate on the most challenging issues facing the world.

Among the very first were the League of Nations, formed in 1919, the 1944 Bretton Woods conference, which established the World Bank and International Monetary Fund, and the United Nations, which replaced the League of Nations in 1945. This multilateral, nation-based approach saw its culmination in the 1992 Rio Earth Summit, where 172 countries were represented, including 108 heads of state or government.

However, various non-political forums have also emerged. One of the first to form was the Club of Rome, a global think-tank founded in 1968 by Aurelio Peccei, an Italian industrialist, and Alexander King, a Scottish scientist. Since its inception, it has regularly brought together scientists, economists, businessmen, international high civil servants, heads of state and former heads of state. Among its most influential reports was *The Limits to Growth*, published in 1972.

The World Economic Forum (WEF) is another such self-organising group, conceived as the European Management Forum in 1971 by management professor Klaus Schwab. Events in 1973, especially the collapse of the Bretton Woods fixed exchange rate mechanism and the Arab–Israeli War, quickly broadened the scope of WEF's annual meetings of executives in Davos to consider economic and social matters, including extending invitations to selected politicians, civil society leaders and social entrepreneurs.

The World Social Forum (WSF) emerged as a reaction against the apparent exclusivity and neoliberal agenda of the World Economic Forum. First held in Porto Alegre in 2001, it has become the annual meeting place of tens of thousands of grassroots, civil society leaders and organisations in various parts of the world.

More recently, we have also seen the formation of some interesting hybrid organisations. For example, the UN Global Compact has held two Leaders Summits (in 2004 and 2007), while the World Economic Forum has spun off the Young Global Leaders Forum, which announces a shortlist 200–300 'extraordinary individuals' who have demonstrated a commitment to serving society and are willing to devote their energy and expertise for five years to tackle the most critical issues facing the world.

Another example of a self-organising forum of leaders is the Prince of Wales's Corporate Leaders Group on Climate Change, which has, since 2005, been urging the UK and EU governments of the need to develop new and longer-term policies for tackling climate change. In 2007, it issued the Bali Communiqué, a public letter by the business leaders of 150 global companies to world leaders calling for a comprehensive, legally binding UN framework to tackle climate change.

1919	League of Nations formed
1944	Bretton Woods conference held
1945	United Nations formed
1971	First meeting of World Economic Forum (then EMF) in Davos
1976	Club of Rome formed
1992	UN Conference on Environment and Development (the 'Earth Summit') held in Rio de Janeiro
2001	First World Social Forum held in Porto Alegre
2004	First UN Global Compact Leaders Summit held in New York
2004	First Young Global Leaders Award announced
2005	Corporate Leaders Group on Climate Change issues first open letter

World Economic Forum

The World Economic Forum (WEF) was first conceived in January 1971 when a group of European business leaders met in Davos, Switzerland, under the patronage of the European Commission and European industrial associations. The meeting was chaired by Klaus Schwab, then Professor of Business Policy at the University of Geneva, who established the group as the European Management Forum (EMF), and renamed it the World Economic Forum in 1987.

Since then, WEF has continued to grow in influence, broadening its scope beyond its members of 'the 1,000 leading companies of the world' to include politicians, civil society leaders and social entrepreneurs. Discussions have also evolved from a narrow focus on business to a broader agenda of social, environmental and economic topics.

WEF's Centre for Strategic Insight issues several flagship reports, including the *Global Competitiveness Report* (published in 1979 and now covering 131 countries), the *Global Gender Gap Report* and *Global Information Technology Report*.

Other activities include WEF's Centre for Public–Private Partnerships, which engages businesses, civil society and political authorities in initiatives ranging from health initiatives in India to alliances combating chronic hunger in Africa. WEF has also spun off other initiatives, such as the Forum of Young Global Leaders, set up in 2004.

FACTBOX

- ▶ At the 1988 WEF meeting, the 'Davos Declaration' was signed by Greece and Turkey, which saw them turn back from the brink of war.
- ▶ In 1989, North and South Korea held their first ministerial-level meetings in Davos, and, at the same meeting, East German Prime Minister Hans Modrow and German Chancellor Helmut Kohl met to discuss German reunification.
- ▶ In 1992, South African President F.W. de Klerk met Nelson Mandela and Chief Mangosuthu Buthelezi at Davos, their first joint appearance outside South Africa and a milestone in the country's political transition.
- ▶ In 2002, a Disaster Resource Network, leveraging engineering and transportation industry firms' resources to assist with disaster relief efforts, was announced, and the Gates Foundation donated US$50 million for AIDS prevention in Africa.
- ▶ In 2007, 49 hours over 24 sessions at WEF were spent addressing environmental issues. Specific initiatives focused on hunger, climate change, energy, corporate citizenship and humanitarian relief.
- ▶ In 2008, Japanese Prime Minister Yasuo Fukuda unveiled a five-year, US$10 billion fund to support efforts in developing countries to combat global warming, and 2 million people took part in an online Davos 'conversation' held on YouTube.

Klaus Schwab,
Founder and Executive
Chairman, World
Economic Forum
World Economic Forum

World Social Forum

The World Social Forum (WSF) first met in Porto Alegre in Brazil in 2001 as an alternative to the World Economic Forum in Davos. It describes itself as an open meeting place where social movements, networks, NGOs and other civil society organisations opposed to neo-liberalism and a world dominated by capital, or by any form of imperialism, come together to pursue their thinking, debate ideas democratically, formulate proposals, share their ex-periences freely and network for effective action.

Hence, the WSF styles itself as a grassroots movement with no clear leadership, other than a committee responsible for organising each annual forum and an International Council which discusses general issues. It aims to facilitate decentralised coordination and net-working among organisations engaged in concrete action towards building another world, at any level from the local to the international, but it does not claim to be a body represent-ing world civil society.

The WSF is guided by a motto — 'another world is possible' — and a Charter of Principles. For example, Article 4 of the Charter states:

- The alternatives proposed at the World Social Forum stand in opposition to a process of globalisation commanded by the large multinational corporations and by the govern-ments and international institutions at the service of those corporations' interests, with the complicity of national governments.

- They are designed to ensure that globalisation in solidarity will prevail as a new stage in world history.

- This will respect universal human rights, and those of all citizens — men and women — of all nations and the environment and will rest on democratic international systems and institutions at the service of social justice, equality and the sovereignty of peo-ples.

FACTBOX

- ▶ The first three WSF meetings were held in Porto Alegre in Brazil in 2001 (with 20,000 attendees), 2002 (50,000 attendees) and 2003 (100,000 attendees).
- ▶ In 2004 it was held in Mumbai, India (75,000 participants) and in 2005 it returned to Porto Alegre (155,000 participants).
- ▶ In 2006, the meeting experimented with a 'polycentric' approach, and was held in three locations: Caracas (Venezuela), Bamako (Mali) and Karachi (Pakistan); in 2007 it was held in Nairobi, Kenya (66,000 attendees).
- ▶ In 2008, it returned to its polycentric model, but took it even further, with thousands of autonomous local organisations convening in different locations around the world.

hing of the World
al Forum, Porto
e, Brazil, 2005
Cardeal

BOOKS

Paul Hawken, *Blessed Unrest: How the Largest Movement in the World Came into Being and Why No One Saw It Coming* (Viking, 2007)

Naomi Klein, *The Shock Doctrine: The Rise of Disaster Capitalism* (Metropolitan Books, 2007)

José Corrêa Leite, *The World Social Forum: Strategies of Resistance* (Haymarket Books, 2005)

Geoffrey Allen Pigman, *The World Economic Forum: A Multi-stakeholder Approach to Global Governance* (Routledge, 2007)

Jai Sen and Peter Waterman (eds.), *World Social Forum: Challenging Empires* (Black Rose Books, new edn, 2009)

Jackie Smith, Marina Karides and Marc Becker, *Global Democracy and the World Social Forums* (Paradigm Publishers, 2007)

Boaventura de Sousa Santos, *The Rise of the Global Left: The World Social Forum and Beyond* (Zed Books, 2006)

Joseph Stiglitz, *Globalization and Its Discontents* (W.W. Norton, 2002)

Joseph Stiglitz, *Making Globalization Work: The Next Steps to Global Justice* (Penguin Allen Lane, 2006)

REPORTS

Bali Communiqué (Prince of Wales's Corporate Leaders Group on Climate Change, 2007)

Global Competitiveness Report 2007–2008 (World Economic Forum)

Global Gender Gap Report 2007 (World Economic Forum)

Global Information Technology Report 2006–2007 (World Economic Forum)

Limits to Growth Report (Club of Rome, 1972)

Poznan Communiqué (Prince of Wales's Corporate Leaders Group on Climate Change, 2008)

Young Global Leaders 2008 (Forum of Young Global Leaders)

WEBSITES

Club of Rome: www.clubofrome.org

Forum of Young Global Leaders: www.younggloballeaders.org

Global Competitiveness Report: www.weforum.org/en/initiatives/gcp

Prince of Wales's Climate Leaders Group: www.cpi.cam.ac.uk/programmes/energy_ and_climate_change/clgcc.aspx

UN Global Compact Leaders Summit 2007: www.globalcompactsummit.org

WiserEarth: www.wiserearth.org

World Economic Forum: www.weforum.org

World Social Forum: www.wsf2008.net

12
SOCIAL ENTERPRISE

We need to reverse three centuries of walling the for-profit and non-profit sectors off from one another. The core psychology of a social entrepreneur is someone who cannot come to rest, in a very deep sense, until he or she has changed the pattern in an area of social concern all across society.

BILL DRAYTON, founder of Ashoka

I like to support causes where 'a lot of good comes from a little bit of good', or, in other words, where the positive social returns vastly exceed the amount of time and money invested.

JEFF SKOLL, first president of eBay

The poor, once economically empowered, are the most determined fighters in the battle to solve the population problem, end illiteracy and live healthier, better lives. When policy makers finally realise that the poor are their partners, rather than bystanders or enemies, we will progress much faster that we do today.

MUHAMMAD YUNUS, founder of the Grameen Bank

Social enterprises have a growing importance. They are increasing local productivity and competitiveness and are promoting neighbourhood regeneration.

PATRICIA HEWITT, former UK Secretary of State for Trade and Industry

A Bamyan weave
the Arzu program
poised at a loom
her ho

Arzu, Inc. is a not-f
profit organisati
providing sustainal
income, educatio
healthcare a
community buildi
programmes
Afghan wom
weavers and th
famil

www.arzurugs.
Thomas Lee for Arzu,

Turning entrepreneurial skills towards solving world problems...

Social enterprises have been around in all but name for many years, stretching back as far as 1844 when, suffering at the hands of exploitative factory owners and shopkeepers who charged extortionate prices, 28 working men in Rochdale in the UK scraped together £28 to open their own shop — so heralding the beginning of the modern cooperative movement.

Shortly thereafter, Franz Hermann Schulze-Delitzsch established the first credit unions in the 1850s in Germany to give those lacking access to financial services the opportunity to borrow from the savings pooled by themselves and their fellow members. Now, the World Council of Credit Unions boasts 172 million members, through 46,000 credit unions in 97 countries.

However, it was only in the 1980s that the modern concept of social enterprise began to come into its own. Among the pioneers was Muhammad Yunus, who started the Grameen Bank as an action research project in 1976 to encourage microfinance among the poor. It became an independent bank in 1983 and, today, it is a $2.5 billion business.

Another was Bill Drayton, who set up Ashoka in Washington, DC in 1981. Since then, it has elected over 1,800 leading social entrepreneurs as Ashoka Fellows, providing them with living stipends, professional support,

1980	Ashoka founded
1983	Grameen Bank registered as an independent bank
1984	FUNDES created
1991	Café Direct founded
1998	Schwab Foundation for Social Entrepreneurship created
1999	Skoll Foundation created
2002	Social Enterprise Alliance formed
2002	UK government launches a Social Enterprise Strategy
2005	International Year of Microcredit
2006	Muhammad Yunus and Grameen Bank awarded the Nobel Peace Prize

and access to a global network of peers in more than 60 countries. Ashoka's budget has grown from $50,000 to nearly $30 million in 2006.

Shortly after Ashoka was founded, in 1984 former Archbishop of Panama Marcos McGrath and Swiss businessman Stephan Schmidheiny set up FUNDES in Panama to provide credit guarantees for small industrial companies. Other sources of funding emerged from the likes of Klaus Schwab, who built on the success of the World Economic Forum, which he started in 1971, by creating the Schwab Foundation for Social Entrepreneurship. Similarly, Jeff Skoll used his eBay fortune to set up the Skoll Foundation.

Today, these and other organisations, such as the Social Enterprise Alliance in the US and the Social Enterprise Network in the UK, act as clearinghouses for knowledge and networking for social entrepreneurs. These social enterprises include organisations such as Café Direct and The Big Issue (both founded in 1991), which have become major forces in promoting fair trade for developing-country farmers and homelessness in the world's cities, respectively.

Government institutions are also seeing the importance of social enterprise. For example, the UN declared 2005 the Year of Microcredit, and the UK government now has a Social Enterprise Strategy. Furthermore, social entrepreneurs and social enterprises are being held up as role models for the rest of society: Muhammad Yunus and Grameen Bank were awarded the Nobel Peace Prize in 2006. Today, we see new start-ups such as Volans Ventures increasingly putting faith in social entrepreneurs to solve the world's social and environmental problems.

Grameen Bank

In 1976, Professor Muhammad Yunus, Head of the Rural Economics Program at the University of Chittagong, launched an action research project, called the Grameen Bank Project, to examine the possibility of designing a credit delivery system to provide banking services targeted at the rural poor.

The project demonstrated its strength in Jobra and was extended to the Tangail district in 1979 and several others thereafter until, in 1983, the Grameen Bank Project was transformed into an independent bank by government legislation.

Grameen Bank targets the poorest of the poor, providing small loans (usually less than $300) to those unable to obtain credit from traditional banks. Loans are administered to groups of five people, with only two receiving their money upfront. As soon as these two make a few regular payments, loans are gradually extended to the rest of the group. In this way, the programme builds a sense of community as well as individual self-reliance.

In 2006, the Nobel Peace Prize was awarded to Muhammad Yunus and the Grameen Bank 'for their efforts to create economic and social development from below'.

Today, the Grameen Bank concept has been extended to other businesses, including GrameenPhone, Grameen Check (loom-woven cloths), Grameen Fisheries Foundation, Grameen Cybernet and Grameen Shakti (energy).

FACTBOX

- Grameen means 'rural' or 'village' in the Bangla language.
- Most of the Grameen Bank's loans are to women, and, since its inception, there has been an astonishing loan repayment rate of over 98%.
- Borrowers from the Bank own 90% of its shares, while the remaining 10% is owned by the government.
- The Grameen Bank is now a $2.5 billion banking enterprise in Bangladesh, with over 7 million active clients, affecting 35 million family members.
- Microfinance advisory services by the International Finance Corporation (IFC) generated over $4.6 billion in new investment financing to over 2.3 million microentrepreneurs in 2006 (equivalent to 15% of the IFC's expenditure).
- According to the Microfinance Summit Campaign, by 2007 there were 3,316 microcredit institutions reaching over 133 million clients; 93 million (up from 7.6 million in 1997) were among the poorest when they took their first loan. Of these poorest clients, 85%, or 79 million, are women.
- The microcredit model has spread to over 50 countries worldwide, from the US and Papua New Guinea to Norway and Nepal.

Muhammad Yunus
Olaf Storbeck

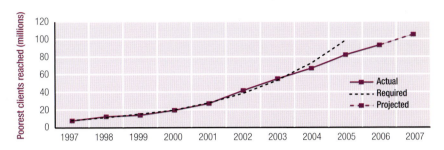

Figure 14 Growth in microfinance reaching the poorest people (1997–2006)
Source: *State of the Microcredit Summit Campaign Report 2007*

Schwab and Skoll Foundations

Schwab Foundation

The Schwab Foundation for Social Entrepreneurship is a non-profit organisation based in Geneva, Switzerland. It was established by Klaus Schwab (President and Founder of the World Economic Forum) and his wife Hilde in 1998 to highlight social entrepreneurship as a key element to advance societies and address social problems in an innovative and effective manner.

The Foundation defines a social entrepreneur as 'A pragmatic visionary who achieves large scale, systemic and sustainable social change through a new invention, a different approach, a more rigorous application of known technologies or strategies, or a combination of these'.

The Foundation suggests that social entrepreneurs share common traits, including:

- An unwavering belief in the innate capacity of all people to contribute meaningfully to economic and social development;
- A driving passion to make that happen;
- A practical but innovative stance to a social problem, often using market principles and forces, coupled with dogged determination;
- A zeal to measure and monitor their impact; and
- A healthy impatience. Social entrepreneurs don't do well in bureaucracies. They cannot sit back and wait for change to happen — they are the change drivers.

The Foundation searches for leading social entrepreneurs around the world and includes them into its network after a thorough due-diligence process. Currently, the network includes 140 social entrepreneurs.

The Foundation runs 'Social Entrepreneur of the Year' competitions in 25 countries and hosts an annual Social Entrepreneurship Summit. Winners of the national competitions are eligible to join the global Schwab Foundation network.

Skoll Foundation

The Skoll Foundation was created by Jeff Skoll, first President of eBay, in 1999 to advance systemic change to benefit communities around the world by investing in, connecting and celebrating social entrepreneurs.

The Foundation invests in social entrepreneurs through its flagship award programme, the Skoll Awards for Social Entrepreneurship. These three-year awards support the continuation, replication or extension of programmes that have proved successful in addressing a broad array of critical social issues.

The Foundation also promotes social entrepreneurship through: the Skoll Centre for Social Entrepreneurship, launched in 2003 at Oxford's Saïd Business School; Social Edge, an on-line community; and the PBS Foundation Social Entrepreneurship Fund, which supports films and documentaries on social entrepreneurship.

The Foundation defines a social entrepreneur as 'society's change agent: pioneer of innovations that benefit humanity'.

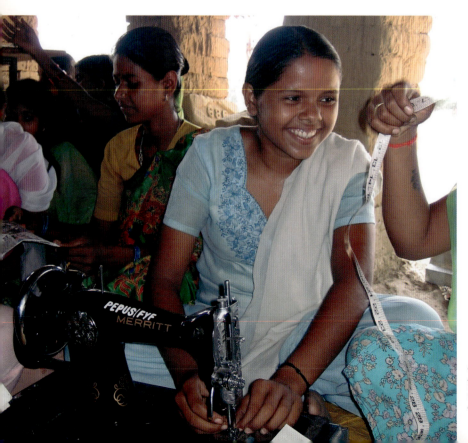

One of Find Your Feet's Adolescent Girls' Education Centres in Uttar Pradesh, India
Catriona Fox, Find Your Feet

BOOKS

David Bornstein, *How to Change the World: Social Entrepreneurs and the Power of New Ideas* (OUP, 2nd edn, 2007)

James Copestake, Martin Greeley, Susan Johnson, Naila Kabeer and Anton Simanowitz, *Money with a Mission. Volume 1: Microfinance and Poverty Reduction* (ITDG Publishing, 2005)

Alex Counts, *Small Loans, Big Dreams: How Nobel Prize Winner Muhammad Yunus and Microfinance are Changing the World* (John Wiley, 2008)

John Elkington and Pamela Hartigan, *The Power of Unreasonable People: How Social Entrepreneurs Create Markets That Change the World* (Harvard Business School Press, 2008)

Philip Smith and Eric Thurman, *A Billion Bootstraps: Microcredit, Barefoot Banking, and the Business Solution for Ending Poverty* (McGraw-Hill Professional, 2007)

Muhammad Yunus, *Banker to the Poor: Micro-lending and the Battle against World Poverty* (Public Affairs, rev. edn, 2003)

Muhammad Yunus, *Creating a World without Poverty: Social Business and the Future of Capitalism* (Public Affairs, paperback edn, 2008)

REPORTS

Everyone a Changemaker: Social Entrepreneurship's Ultimate Goal (Bill Drayton, 2006)

Fostering Social Entrepreneurship: A Comparative Study of the Legal, Regulatory and Tax Issues in Brazil, Germany, India, Poland, UK and USA (Schwab Foundation, 2006)

Growing Opportunity: Entrepreneurial Solutions to Insoluble Problems (SustainAbility, 2007)

Knowing History, Serving It: Ashoka's Theory of Change (William Drayton, 2003)

Market Based Solutions for Financing Philanthropy (Arthur Wood and Maximilian Martin, 2006)

Measuring Innovation: Evaluation in the Field of Social Entrepreneurship (Mark R. Kramer/FSG and Skoll Foundation, 2005)

Scaling Capacities: Supports for Growing Impact (LaFrance Associates and Skoll Foundation, 2006)

The State of the Microcredit Summit Campaign Report 2007 (Microcredit Summit Campaign, 2007)

WEBSITES

Ashoka: www.ashoka.org

The Big Issue: www.bigissue.com

Café Direct: www.cafedirect.co.uk

The Co-operative Group: www.co-operative.co.uk

The Eden Project: www.edenproject.com

FUNDES: www.fundes.org/Eng

Grameen Bank: www.grameen-info.org

Microcredit Summit Campaign: www.microcreditsummit.org

Schwab Foundation for Social Entrepreneurship: www.schwabfound.org

Skoll Centre for Social Entrepreneurship: www.sbs.ox.ac.uk/skoll

Skoll Foundation: www.skollfoundation.org

Social Edge: www.socialedge.org

Social Enterprise Alliance: www.se-alliance.org

Social Enterprise Coalition: www.socialenterprise.org.uk

Volans Ventures: www.volans.com

IV

COLLABORATION

13
INDUSTRY INITIATIVES

The Forest Stewardship Council exemplifies an environmental and social NGO at the centre of an exceptional and innovative partnership among business, the public sector, and civil society to raise business standards.

ROBERT DAVIES, former Chief Executive Officer of the International Business Leaders Forum

At this point, we cannot support anyone purchasing palm oil because it is Roundtable for Sustainable Palm Oil (RSPO) certified — the realities are that this certification is not nearly strong enough to be considered 'sustainable'.

BRIHANNALA C. MORGAN, Rainforest Agribusiness Campaigner for Rainforest Action Network

The challenge is 'trust'. How do we make our stakeholders feel confident in the fact that the chemical industry really is implementing Responsible Care? This re-opens the debate about management systems, self-assessment and ways to achieve some 'external certification'.

JEAN-PAUL PERES, Chairman, Responsible Care Strategy Implementation Group

It is consumer power that drives the Marine Stewardship Council. The organisation enables individuals, literally around the world, to make individual choices about sustainability.

HRH THE PRINCE OF WALES

Birds and pollut
Jeff Chevrier/istockpl

When collaboration is better than competition . . .

The response of industry sectors to sustainability issues has evolved and matured considerably in the past 20 years. The first sector to form a coordinated view was the chemical industry, which established Responsible Care in 1985. This was, even by their own admission, a defensive attempt to restore trust in the industry, following a spate of industrial accidents such as Bhopal.

The next major initiative came in the financial sector, with the establishment of the United Nations Environment Programme (UNEP) Finance Initiative. This partnership between the UN and many of the world's largest financial institutions marked the beginning of a more collaborative (and, some would say, credible) approach. UNEP FI has subsequently been instrumental in other sector initiatives such as the Equator Principles and the UN Principles for Responsible Investment.

Building on this partnership approach, the Forest Stewardship Council (FSC), which was set up in 1993, quickly became the exemplar for how to create a stakeholder-inclusive sector standard. Despite some resistance from the industry (or perhaps even because of it), FSC has enjoyed high levels of public trust and growing success. Today, it is the most rapidly growing forestry certification standard and is widely regarded as a benchmark for good practice.

One spin-off of the FSC was its sister organisation, the Marine Stewardship Council (MSC), set up in 1997 and supported from the outset by companies such as Unilever. The decision in 2006 by Wal-Mart to adopt the standard has turned it from a marginal to a mainstream sector response.

Other agricultural sector initiatives include the 2001 Cocoa Protocol and the Roundtable on Sustainable Palm Oil, established in 2003. Palm oil, which is already present in one in ten supermarket products, is seen as a major player in the future biofuels market, prompting serious concerns about associated deforestation. The success of the Roundtable is therefore regarded as crucial.

Other sector responses have had mixed success. The Sustainable Development Charter of the International Council on Mining & Metals — which grew out of the 2002 Mining and Minerals for Sustainable Development (MMSD) project — has hardly been recognised outside the industry.

In contrast, the Kimberley Process to stop trade in conflict diamonds, which introduced its certification scheme in 2002, and the Extractive Industries Transparency Initiative, begun in 2003, have both been seen as high-profile success stories by their sectors.

Various other sector initiatives — such as those of the WBCSD in cement, mobility and tyres, or the travel and tourism industry's series of codes, declarations and standards — have yet to prove their impacts. What is clear, however, is that sector-based responses to sustainability, if they adopt a stakeholder-driven approach, are perhaps the best way to bring about substantive change.

1985 Responsible Care launched

1992 UN Environment Programme (UNEP) Banking Initiative launched

1993 Forest Stewardship Council (FSC) established

1994 Green Globe standard for travel and tourism launched

1997 Marine Stewardship Council (MSC) established

1997 UNEP Insurance Industry Initiative (III) formed

1999 Cement Sustainability Initiative launched

2000 Mining and Minerals for Sustainable Development (MMSD) project started

2000 Kimberley Process to stop trade in conflict diamonds initiative launched

2003 Roundtable on Sustainable Palm Oil created

Responsible Care

Responsible Care is a voluntary chemical sector initiative to continuously improve the environmental, health and safety knowledge and performance of the sector's technologies, processes and products over their life-cycles.

Responsible Care was started in Canada in 1985, and is now active in 53 countries around the world under the umbrella of the International Council of Chemical Associations (ICCA), accounting for nearly 90% of global chemicals production.

Responsible Care requires the management, measurement, reporting and verification of performance on: community awareness, employee health and safety at work, process safety, protection of the environment, product stewardship, emergency response, waste reduction, safe warehousing and distribution, environment, transportation, product stewardship, and physical security of facilities and systems.

As part of the Global Strategic Review of Responsible Care, an External Stakeholder Survey conducted by SustainAbility in 2004 concluded that:

- The industry is perceived by many as a 'necessary evil', one that makes products that improve lives, but which also poses both a near-term and long-term threat to the health and well-being of the public and the environment.

- Industry strengths include technical expertise and availability of resources to manage the risk associated with its operations.

- Weaknesses include a lack of transparency and engagement, lack of accountability and common metrics, a poor understanding of product risks, and a bifurcation between the performance of large companies and that of medium and small companies.

In response, the Responsible Care Global Charter was launched in 2006 as an agreement achieved among the members of the ICCA to create a common global vision for Responsible Care among the nations that implement the initiative.

FACTBOX

▶ Responsible Care signatory chemical organisations represent over 1 million employees worldwide.

▶ Over 90% of Responsible Care programmes around the world have fully established sets of safety, health and environmental performance indicators, and around 80% are making these figures available to the public.

▶ Nearly 80% of Responsible Care associations internationally have fully implemented product stewardship into their programme.

▶ Between 2000 and 2005, the number of chemical sector fatalities reported across 34 countries halved from 56 to 28.

▶ Between 2000 and 2005, the ratio of distribution incidents (accidents, spillages, etc.) to millions of tonnes distributed dropped from 7.9 to 1.2.

▶ In 2005, the chemical industry across 30 countries reported direct CO_2 emissions of 450 million tonnes and indirect CO_2 emissions of 86 million tonnes.

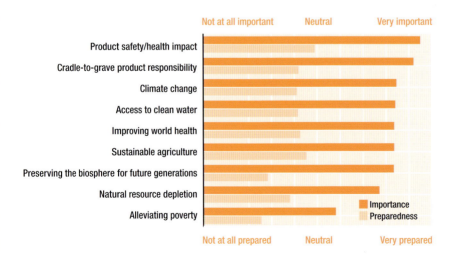

Figure 15 **Sustainable development issues: industry importance and preparedness**

Source: SustainAbility, *External Stakeholder Survey: Final Report for the Global Strategic Review of Responsible Care®* (Washington, DC: SustainAbility, February 2004)

Man-made fires to clear land for cattle or crops, São Felix Do Xingu Municipality, Pará, Brazil

© Greenpeace/Daniel Béltra

Forest Stewardship Council (FSC)

The origins of the Forest Stewardship Council (FSC) date back to a meeting of a group of timber users, traders and environmental and human rights organisations in California in 1990 who had identified the need for an honest and credible system for identifying well-managed forests as acceptable sources of forest products.

The result was the FSC, formally established in 1993 to promote responsible stewardship of the world's forests, and now an international organisation operating through a network of National Initiatives in 45 countries.

The FSC sets international standards for responsible forest management and accredits independent third-party organisations who can certify forest managers and forest product producers to FSC standards.

PEFC (Programme for the Endorsement of Forest Certification schemes) is the main competing forest certification system, established by the forest industry in response to the creation and increasing popularity of FSC.

The Sustainable Furniture Council (SFC) is a non-profit industry association founded at High Point, NC, in October 2006 to promote sustainable practices among manufacturers, retailers and consumers alike.

FACTBOX

▶ More than 94 million hectares in over 78 countries are now certified to FSC standards. This represents the equivalent of 7% of forests identified primarily for production.

▶ FSC is the fastest-growing forest certification scheme, with 20 million hectares added in 2006 (a 33% increase) and nearly 10 million added in 2007.

▶ Since the end of the 1990s, rates of primary forest loss have increased in the tropics. Between 2000 and 2005, deforestation rates of primary forest rose 25.6% (from 0.67% per year to 0.84% annually) for the 17 countries with the most significant forest resources.

▶ Between 1990 and 2005, the world lost over 10 million hectares of forest annually across 62 countries; 28% of this annual loss occurred in Brazil.

▶ The Leadership Council for the Book Industry Treatise on Responsible Paper has a goal of shifting the book industry's collective average use of paper certified by the Forest Stewardship Council system to 20% and increasing the use of recycled paper fibre to 30% by 2012.

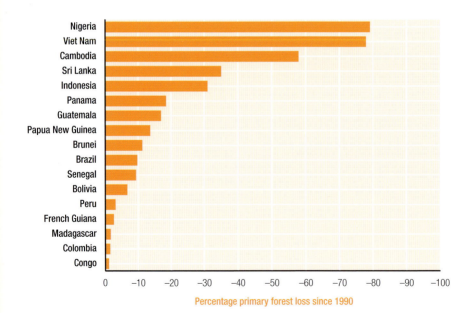

Percentage primary forest loss since 1990

Figure 16 **Tropical deforestation by region (1990–2005)**

Source: www.mongabay.com

REPORTS

Breaking New Ground: The Report of the Mining, Minerals and Sustainable Development Project (International Institute for Environment and Development [IIED], 2002)

Climate Change and Tourism Responding to Global Challenges: Davos Declaration (Second International Conference on Climate Change and Tourism, 2007)

External Stakeholder Survey: Global Strategic Review of Responsible Care (SustainAbility, 2004)

Facts and Figures on FSC Growth and Markets (Forest Stewardship Council [FSC], 2008)

Global Forest Resources Assessment 2005: Progress towards Sustainable Forest Management (Food and Agriculture Organisation of the United Nations [FAO])

Greasy Palms: Palm Oil, the Environment and Big Business (Friends of the Earth, 2004)

ICCA Responsible Care Status Report 2007 (International Council of Chemical Associations [ICCA])

The Kimberley Process Certification Scheme: Third Year Review (Kimberley Process, 2006)

Marine Stewardship Council Annual Report 2006/07 (Marine Stewardship Council [MSC], 2007)

Mobility 2030: Meeting the Challenges to Sustainability (World Business Council for Sustainable Development [WBCSD], 2004)

Powering a Sustainable Future: An Agenda for Concerted Action (World Business Council for Sustainable Development [WBCSD], 2006)

Responsible Tourism in Destinations: The Cape Town Declaration (2002)

Sustainable Palm Oil: Good Agricultural Practice Guidelines (Unilever, 2003)

Towards a Sustainable Cement Industry (Battelle and World Business Council for Sustainable Development [WBCSD], 2002)

UNEP Finance Initiative 2006 Overview (UNEP Finance Initiative [FI], 2006)

WEBSITES

Cement Sustainability Initiative: www.wbcsdcement.org

Forest Stewardship Council: www.fsc.org

International Council on Mining and Metals: www.icmm.com

Kimberley Process: www.kimberleyprocess.com

Marine Stewardship Council: www.msc.org

Mining, Minerals and Sustainable Development: www.iied.org/mmsd

Responsible Care: www.responsiblecare.org

Roundtable on Sustainable Palm Oil: www.rspo.org

UNEP Finance Initiative: www.unepfi.org

UN FAO Forestry webpage: www.fao.org/forestry

WBCSD Sector Projects: www.wbcsd.org

World Federation of the Sporting Goods Industry: www.wfsgi.org

14
FINANCIAL INITIATIVES

Consideration of environmental, social and corporate governance factors are essential to prudent investment management and therefore essential to the fiduciary responsibility of pension fund trustees and investment managers.

CARLOS JOLY, Co-chair of the UNEP FI Asset Management Working Group

The revised Equator Principles definitely add to making the financing of globalisation much more socially responsible. It proves the positive convergence of public and private engagement in safeguarding progress on the road to a more civil world.

LARS KOLTE, Managing Director of EKF and Chairman of the Council of Europe Development Bank

The Equator Principles, as a voluntary set of principles, will be meaningless unless independent monitoring and compliance mechanisms are put in place. Signatories cannot expect to receive much public credit without accountability procedures that ensure that these banks practise what they preach on the ground.

BRUCE RICH, Director of the International Program at Environmental Defense

We know that loans to small and micro businesses can help grow more equitable economies. Yet, the world over, access to credit for smaller borrowers is scarce to nonexistent. We all have a stake in creating more inclusive economies. Fostering local financial institutions which provide credit in their communities will help make this happen.

JAMES WOLFENSOHN, former President of the World Bank

Swiss Re Tower in
City of Lond
istockp

Turning financial risks into opportunities . . .

Ethical finance is an umbrella term for the activities of financial institutions that take social, environmental and ethical considerations into account. An early manifestation of this was the scrutiny that banks were subject to in the 1970s and 1980s with regard to their investments in apartheid South Africa and their complicity in Third World debt.

In the 1990s, the indirect environmental impacts of banks were increasingly placed under the spotlight, and the industry responded in the lead-up to the Rio Earth Summit by issuing the United Nations Environment Programme (UNEP) Statement by Banks on the Environment and Sustainable Development and establishing the UNEP Banking Initiative. This was followed in 1995 with the UNEP Statement of Environmental Commitment for the Insurance Industry and in 1997 with the establishment of the Insurance Industry Initiative. Eventually, in 2003, the Banking and Insurance Initiatives merged to form the UNEP Finance Initiative.

Meanwhile, climate change was rising up the world's agenda, and the financial implications were starting to become clear. In order to improve the information required by the financial sector to begin factoring in climate risks, the Carbon Disclosure Project (CDP) was set up in 2000. Today, the CDP provides a coordinating secretariat for institutional investors with a combined $57 trillion of assets under management. On their behalf it seeks information on the business risks and opportunities presented by climate change

1992	UNEP Statement by Banks launched
1995	UNEP Statement by the Insurance Sector launched
2000	Carbon Disclosure Project launched
2002	London Principles launched at the WSSD
2003	UNEP Finance Initiative created
2003	Equator Principles launched (revised in 2006)
2004	World Bank Extractive Industries Review completed
2006	UN Principles for Responsible Investment launched
2007	UNEP Declaration on Climate Change issued
2007	ClimateWise Principles for insurance launched

and greenhouse gas emissions data from the world's largest companies: these numbered 3,000 in 2008.

It soon became clear that the finance sector needed something with more teeth than the UNEP statements to satisfy its external critics and properly manage the internal risks associated with the social and environmental impacts of its clients. The first development to emerge was the London Principles, which were launched at the Johannesburg World Summit on Sustainable Development in 2002.

These were followed in 2003 by the launch of the Equator Principles, which focused specifically on project finance. The following year, the World Bank concluded a two-year review of its activities in the extractive industries sector, paying particular attention to the concerns expressed by environmental and human rights organi-

sations. Then 2006 saw the revision of the Equator Principles, broadening their inclusion criteria, and the launch of the UN Principles for Responsible Investment.

We will probably look back at 2007 as the tipping point in the climate change debate, and the financial sector's response is no exception. It launched a flurry of initiatives, including the UNEP Declaration on Climate Change, the ClimateWise Principles for the insurance sector, and the P8 Group for the pensions sector.

Individual companies have also taken the initiative, with projects such as Vodafone's M-PESA in Kenya, which allows funds transfers by mobile text in a population where the majority of people do not have bank accounts, or Barclays' microfinance efforts in Ghana, which have been particularly successful.

UNEP Finance Initiative

The concept behind the United Nations Environment Programme Finance Initiative (UNEP FI) was developed in 1991 when a small group of commercial banks, including Deutsche Bank, HSBC Holdings, NatWest, Royal Bank of Canada and Westpac, joined forces with UNEP to catalyse the banking industry's awareness of the environmental agenda.

In May 1992, in the run-up to the Rio Summit that year, the UNEP Statement by Banks on the Environment and Sustainable Development was launched and the Banking Initiative was formed. This was supplemented by the UNEP Statement of Environmental Commitment for the Insurance Industry, launched in 1995.

In 1997, the Insurance Industry Initiative was formed to fund research activities, and to sponsor awareness meetings and workshops and the annual regular meetings of the Initiative. This same year, the UNEP Statement by Banks was redrafted to broaden its appeal, and the Banking Initiative was renamed the Financial Institutions Initiative.

From 1999, both the Financial Institutions Initiative and Insurance Industry Initiative started to work more closely together on issues of mutual interest, and UNEP FI's core working groups were formed: the Climate Change Working Group, the Asset Management Working Group, and the Environmental Management and Reporting Working Group.

In 2003, the UNEP Financial Institutions Initiative and the UNEP Insurance Industry Initiative merged under the banner of the UNEP Finance Initiative. Today, UNEP FI works closely with financial institutions who are signatories to the UNEP FI Statements and a range of partner organisations to develop and promote linkages between the environment, sustainability and financial performance.

Through regional activities, a comprehensive work programme, training programmes and research, UNEP FI carries out its mission to identify, promote and realise the adoption of best environmental and sustainability practice at all levels of financial institution operations.

Its core activities are organised around the following themes: climate change; insurance; investment; property; and sustainability management and reporting.

FACTBOX

▶ Over 160 financial institutions from around the globe are signatories to the principles outlined in the UNEP FI Statements.
▶ By signing the Statements, signatories:
- Acknowledge the various roles of industry and government in promoting sustainable development, and pledge to work together to achieve this goal.
- As appropriate to their specific business, signatories pledge to increase environmental responsibility in their internal operations, risk assessment and management, and asset management.
- Commit themselves to promoting these objectives to the broader community.

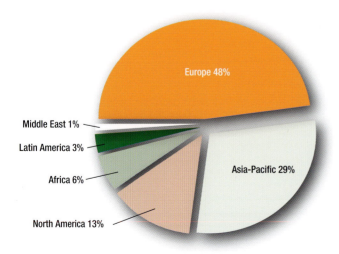

Figure 17 **UNEP FI Statement signatories by region**
Source: UNEP Finance Initiative

Equator Principles

In October 2002, a small number of banks convened in London, together with the World Bank Group's International Finance Corporation (IFC), to develop a global set of environmental and social policies and guidelines for project finance. The result was the Equator Principles, launched in Washington, DC, on 4 June 2003.

In 2006, the IFC reviewed and replaced its existing Environmental and Social Safeguard Policies with new Performance Standards. Since the Equator Principles were based on the Safeguard Policies, they were also revised and reissued in July 2006 to be consistent with the new Performance Standards.

The ten principles include the following commitments for all projects above $10 million in capital costs:

- Ensuring a social and environmental impact assessment is carried out by the borrower and that measures are taken to mitigate any issues that appear;

- Employing a free and open consultation process;

- Commissioning an independent social or environmental review of the project and consultation process; and

- Reporting annually on progress in implementing the Principles.

Equator Principles Financial Institutions (EPFIs) follow three basic steps:

- Categorising all projects from all countries and sectors into high, medium and low environmental and social risk, based on the IFC's categorisation process;

- Requiring borrowers to demonstrate in their Social and Environmental Assessments, and in their Action Plans, the extent to which they have met the applicable World Bank and IFC sector-specific Environment, Health & Safety (EHS) Guidelines and IFC Performance Standards, or to justify deviations from them; and

- Inserting into the loan documentation for high- and medium-risk projects covenants for borrowers to comply with the Action Plan. Where a borrower is not in compliance with its social and environmental covenants, EPFIs either work with the borrower to bring it back into compliance or exercise remedies, as they consider appropriate.

FACTBOX

▶ When the Principles were launched, the original ten signatory banks — including ABN AMRO Bank, N.V., Barclays plc, Citigroup, Inc., Crédit Lyonnais, Credit Suisse First Boston, HVB Group, Rabobank Group, The Royal Bank of Scotland, WestLB AG, and Westpac Banking Corporation — collectively represented approximately $14.5 billion of project loans, or 30% of the project loan syndication market globally in 2002.

▶ As of January 2008, the Principles had been signed by 56 project finance institutions to date representing over 85% of project finance funding worldwide.

The centre of British finance: the Bank of England to the left and the old London Stock Exchange to the right

Chris Schmidt/istockphoto

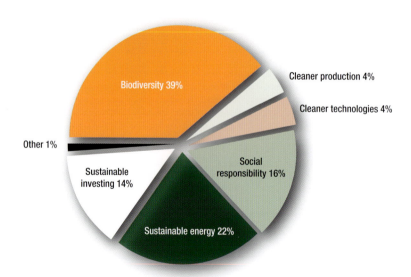

Biodiversity 39%

Cleaner production 4%

Cleaner technologies 4%

Other 1%

Social responsibility 16%

Sustainable investing 14%

Sustainable energy 22%

Figure 18 **International Finance Corporation (IFC) social and environmental sustainability expenditure (2007)**

Source: *International Finance Corporation Annual Report 2007*

BOOKS

Marcel Jeucken, *Sustainability in Finance: Banking on the Planet* (Eburon, 2005)

Marguerite S. Robinson, *The Microfinance Revolution: Sustainable Finance for the Poor — Lessons from Indonesia, the Emerging Industry* (World Bank Publications, 2001)

Muhammad Yunus, *Banker to the Poor: Micro-lending and the Battle against World Poverty* (Public Affairs, rev. edn, 2003)

Malcolm Harper (ed.), *Microfinance: Evolution, Achievement and Challenges* (ITDG Publishing, new edn, 2003)

Rory Sullivan and Craig McKenzie (eds.), *Responsible Investment* (Greenleaf Publishing, 2006)

Jan Jaap Bouma, Marcel Jeucken and Leon Klinkers (eds.), *Sustainable Banking: The Greening of Finance* (Greenleaf Publishing, 2001)

REPORTS

Collevecchio Declaration on Financial Institutions and Sustainability (2003)

Financial Sector Responsibility: The State of the Art (Ethical Corporation, 2006)

Financing the Future: The London Principles (The Role of UK Financial Services in Sustainable Development) (Corporation of London, 2002)

Insuring for Sustainability: Why and How the Leaders Are Doing It (UNEP Finance Initiative, 2004)

The Materiality of Social, Environmental and Corporate Governance Issues to Equity Pricing (UNEP Finance Initiative, 2004)

Principles, Profits, or Just PR? Triple P Investments under the Equator Principles (BankTrack, 2004)

Shaping the Future of Sustainable Finance: Moving the Banking Sector from Promises to Performance (WWF-UK, 2006)

WEBSITES

BankTrack: www.banktrack.org

Carbon Disclosure Project: www.cdproject.net

ClimateWise: www.climatewise.org.uk

The Equator Principles: www.equator-principles.com

P8 Group on climate change for the pensions sector: www.cpi.cam.ac.uk/programmes/energy_and_climate_change/p8_group.aspx

UNEP Finance Initiative: www.unepfi.org

UN Principles for Responsible Investment: www.unpri.org

World Bank: www.worldbank.org

15

SUSTAINABLE INVESTMENT

We're better insulated than the S&P 500 would be, because of the type of companies our social criteria lead us away from... Social criteria take you away from rust-bucket America.

AMY DOMINI, co-founder of the Domini Social Index

We don't think it's acceptable to force a choice between investing according to our values or according to the ways most likely to get us the best return on investment.

AL GORE, former US Vice President,
and co-founder of Generation Investment

Welcome to the future — today. Following on the heels of the computer, Internet, and biotech revolutions, 'clean tech' is bringing unprecedented opportunities for wealth creation, high-growth career development, and innovative solutions to a range of global problems.

RON PERNICK and **CLINT WILDER**,
authors of *The Clean Tech Revolution*

Every day we see closer links between the financial materiality of sustainability issues such as climate change, and the fiduciary duties of those responsible for our companies, capital markets and critical societal investment vehicles.

ACHIM STEINER, UN Under-Secretary General
and UNEP Executive Director

Putting your money where your values are...

The responsible investment phenomenon first became visible in the 1970s when church and university groups set up funds and campaigns to avoid investment in companies supporting the Vietnam War and the apartheid regime in South Africa. Among the most influential at the time were the Pax World Fund, launched in 1971, and the Sullivan Principles, set up by Reverend Leon Sullivan in 1977 to encourage ethical practices by US companies in South Africa.

While these cause-related initiatives continued to exert influence through the 1980s, it was only in 1990 that responsible investment engaged mainstream financial markets, with the launch of the Domini 400 Social Index in the US. This marked the birth of the modern movement, with its three-pronged strategy to bring about change through negative and positive investment screening and shareholder activism.

During the 1990s, the most active market seemed to be the UK, with ethical investment, or socially responsible investment (SRI) as it was often called, being championed by new organisations such as the UK Social Investment Forum. Progressive companies such as Friends Provident led the way, the latter setting up the Stewardship Fund, supported by the Ethical Investment Research Service (EIRIS).

The momentum swung back to the US again, when the Dow Jones launched its

1971	Pax World Fund launched in the USA
1977	Sullivan Principles launched
1990	Domini 400 Social Index launched in the USA
1991	UK Social Investment Forum (UKSIF) established
1999	Dow Jones Sustainability Index launched in the USA
2001	FTSE4Good Index launched in the UK
2002	London Principles of sustainable finance launched
2003	Carbon Disclosure Project (CDP) launched
2004	JSE Socially Responsible Investment Index launched in South Africa
2006	UN Principles for Responsible Investment (PRI) launched

Sustainability Index in 1999, although it adopted a more inclusive approach of 'best-in-sector' rankings, rather than industry exclusions. The London Securities Exchange followed suit with the FTSE4Good Index in 2001, sticking to the European positive and negative screening approach.

The two most significant developments since then have been the creation of similar indexes in emerging economies such as South Africa, Brazil, Malaysia and Singapore, and the rise of climate change as an investment issue. In order to support the financial analysts' information needs of the move towards a low-carbon economy, initiatives such as the Carbon Disclosure Project, launched in 2003, have been critical.

Then, as the scientific certainty about climate change increased in 2006 and 2007, so-called clean-tech investment boomed. Some of this was fuelled by government-created renewable energy funds, but a good deal has also come from venture capitalists and multinational companies betting on a future of cleaner, low-carbon technologies.

The net result, symbolised by the launch of the UN's Principles for Responsible Investment in 2006, is that responsible investment has gone mainstream, with estimates that around 10% of global investments are now selected on the basis of social, ethical or environmental criteria.

Sustainability indexes

The Domini 400 Social Index, launched by KLD Research & Analytics in 1990, was the world's first ethical or social responsibility investment index. Selecting primarily from the S&P 500, the Index screens out tobacco, alcohol, gambling, firearms, military weapons and nuclear power companies, and then selects companies that have positive environmental, social and governance (ESG) performance.

KLD has since introduced various other indexes, including a Catholic Values 400 Index, Global Sustainability Index and Global Climate 100 Index, which together represent more than $11 billion invested.

Launched in 1999, the Dow Jones Sustainability Index (DJSI) follows a 'best-in-class' approach comprising those identified as the sustainability leaders in each industry. Companies are assessed against environmental, social and economic criteria which are industry-specific, so that they are compared against their peers and ranked accordingly. The DJSI's 60 licences held by asset managers in 15 countries presently manage over US$5 billion.

Since their inception, the Domini 400 Index and DJSI have shown cumulative performance above the S&P 500 and Dow Jones Index respectively.

The FTSE4Good Index, launched in 2001, avoids investing in sectors such as tobacco, defence and nuclear power, and applies positive criteria for environmental sustainability, stakeholder relationships, human rights, supply chain labour standards and countering bribery.

The first emerging-market index was the JSE SRI Index in South Africa in 2004, with Brazil, Malaysia and others following suit.

FACTBOX

▶ By July 2007, the 190 signatories of the UN Principles for Responsible Investment (PRI) represented over US$9 trillion in assets under management.

▶ In the USA, one of every nine dollars under professional management is tied to socially responsible investment (SRI), which means $2.71 trillion in total managed assets using a core SRI strategy. Total screened funds rose to $201.8 billion in 2007 from $179 billion in 2005.

▶ In Europe, the SRI market was estimated in 2006 to be up to €1 trillion and representing as much as 10–15% of total European funds under management. This represents a 36% growth since 2002.

▶ In Asia-Pacific in 2006, almost US$24 billion was invested in around 163 SRI mutual funds (unit trusts), with 17 other SRI funds worth around US$8.3 billion, a total of 180 funds worth around US$32.3 billion.

Figure 19 **Domini 400 Social Index cumulative performance (1990–2008)**
Source: KLD

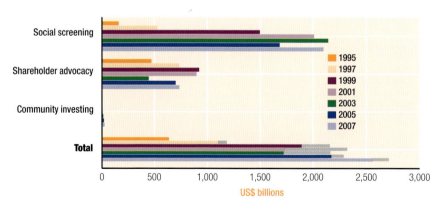

Note. Overlapping assets involved in 'social screening' and 'shareholder advocacy' have been subtracted from the total to avoid potential double-counting (the subtracted amount is visible in the underlying grey bars in the 'total' area).

Figure 20 **Socially responsible investment in the US (1995–2007)**
Source: Social Investment Forum, *2007 Report on Socially Responsible Investing Trends in the United States: Executive Summary* (Washington, DC: Social Investment Forum)

Clean-tech investment

The trend of clean-tech investment has its roots in the environmental technology or 'green-tech' movement of the 1970s and 1980s. However, while these tended to be highly regulation-driven and 'end-of-pipe' with limited returns, clean-tech is now market-driven with significant financial and sustainability benefits.

Reflecting this trend, in 2007 the London Accord was launched, bringing the innovation and rigour of financial markets' research to bear on the evaluation of investment opportunities in potential solutions to the impact, and mitigation, of climate change. The London Accord partners have created a reference guide to:

• Better measure links between investment, finance and 'carbon' returns; and
• Better understand interactions between public policy and investment decisions.

According to Ron Pernick and Clint Wilder of Clean Edge, clean-tech can be defined as any product, service or process that delivers value using limited or zero non-renewable resources and/or creates significantly less waste than conventional offerings.

Pernick and Wilder identify six forces behind the rapid growth of clean-tech: falling clean energy costs and rising fossil fuel prices; capital injection; national competition to become the clean-tech 'Silicon Valley'; China's booming economy and environmental concerns; consumer demand; and climate change.

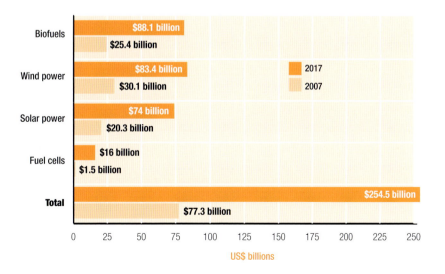

Figure 21 **Global projected clean energy growth (2007–2017)**
Source: Clean Edge, *Clean Energy Trends 2008* (© 2008 Clean Edge, Inc., www.cleanedge.com)

FACTBOX

- ▶ $148.4 billion was invested in clean energy companies and projects in 2007, up 60% from 2006. New investment in clean energy was $33.4 billion in 2004, rising to $92.6 billion in 2006.

- ▶ Venture capital and private equity investment in clean energy companies was up 34% in 2007 to $9.8 billion, while finance via public markets was up more than 123%, thanks in part to the record-breaking IPO (initial public offering) of Iberdrola Renovables, which raised €4 billion ($6 billion) in December. Asset financing was up 68% to $84.5 billion.

- ▶ Annual revenue for four benchmark clean technologies — solar photovoltaics, wind power, biofuels and fuel cells — increased nearly 40% from $40 billion in 2005 to $55 billion in 2006. Clean Edge forecasts that this trajectory will continue and generate a $226 billion market by 2016.

- ▶ Japan is planning to invest up to $1.93 billion in an international fund aimed at encouraging the use of renewable energy technology in developing countries. The fund, set up jointly with the United States and Britain, is expected be the largest ever of its type, with total investment of about $4.82 billion.

plant at 3,000 m
rd Weber/istockphoto

BOOKS

Amy L. Domini, *Socially Responsible Investing: Making a Difference and Making Money* (Kaplan Business, 2000)

John Hancock (ed.), *An Investor's Guide to Ethical and Socially Responsible Investment Funds* (Kogan Page, 2005)

Peter D. Kinder, Amy L. Domini and Steven Lydenberg, *Investing for Good: Making Money While Being Socially Responsible* (HarperBusiness, 1993)

Steven Lydenberg, *Corporations and the Public Interest: Guiding the Invisible Hand* (Berrett-Koehler, 2005)

Ron Pernick and Clint Wilder, *The Clean Tech Revolution: The Next Big Growth and Investment Opportunity* (Collins, 2007)

Russell Sparkes, *Socially Responsible Investment: A Global Revolution* (John Wiley, 2002)

Rory Sullivan and Craig McKenzie (eds.), *Responsible Investment* (Greenleaf Publishing, 2006)

REPORTS

2007 Report on Socially Responsible Investing Trends in the United States (Social Investment Forum [SIF], 2008)

Clean Energy Trends 2008 (Clean Edge, 2008)

The Cleantech Report™ (Lux Research, 2007)

European SRI Study 2006 (Eurosif, 2007)

Partnership: Clean Technology Global Trends and Insights Report 2007 (Ernst & Young, 2008)

Renewables Information 2007 (International Energy Agency [IEA])

Venture Capital for Sustainability 2007 (Eurosif)

WEBSITES

Association for Sustainable & Responsible Investment in Asia (ASrIA): www.asria.org

Carbon Disclosure Project: www.cdproject.net

Clean Edge: www.cleanedge.com

Cleantech Group: www.cleantechnetwork.com

Ethical Investment Research Service (EIRIS): www.eiris.org

European Social Investment Forum (Eurosif): www.eurosif.org

KLD Research & Analytics, Inc.: www.kld.com

New Energy Finance: www.newenergyfinance.com

One Report: www.one-report.com

Social Investment Forum: www.socialinvest.org

Sustainable Investment Research International Ltd (SiRi Company): www.siricompany.com

SRI Asia: www.sri-asia.com

UK Social Investment Forum (UKSIF): www.uksif.org

UN Principles for Responsible Investment: www.unpri.org

16
SUSTAINABLE CONSUMERISM

Every day, whether we are shopping for simple necessities or for luxury items, for fish fingers or fur coats, we are making choices that affect the environmental quality of the world we live in.

JOHN ELKINGTON and **JULIA HAILES,**
authors of *The Green Consumer Guide*

The truth is that our combined best efforts have not been good enough to arrest the alarming decline in real wages, the excessive working hours and the growth in vulnerable employment relationships. Although individual companies have made headway against these trends, conditions for many workers remain poor.

ALAN ROBERTS, chair of the Ethical Trading Initiative (ETI)

Consumers have not been told effectively enough that they have huge power and that purchasing and shopping involve a moral choice.

ANITA RODDICK, Founder, The Body Shop International

Goods produced under conditions which do not meet a rudimentary standard to decency should be regarded as contraband and not allowed to pollute the channels of international commerce.

FRANKLIN D. ROOSEVELT, former US President

Fairtrade chocol
Christian Guthier/Ox

Counting the cost of cheap goods...

There is a long and proud history of campaigning against trade injustices. For example, women's rights and anti-slavery campaigner Mary Wollstonecraft declared in 1792: 'Is one half of the human species, like the poor African slaves, to be subject to prejudices that brutalise them ... only to sweeten the cup of men?' At the time, more than 300,000 people joined a boycott of sugar grown on plantations using slave labour.

This kind of self-organised consumer action continues to this day, with numerous campaigns to boycott products, companies and countries that are claimed to be violating acceptable social and environmental norms. For example, the UK's Ethical Consumer Research Organisation maintains a list of current, active boycotts with registered headquarters. These numbered 54 in February 2008.

In parallel to this consumer boycott tradition, there has also been a movement seeking to visibly identify those products that meet high social and environmental criteria. This has chiefly been through ethically oriented product labelling. Among the pioneers of this trend were the Soil Association, which published its first organic food standards in 1967, followed by Germany's Blue Angel label in 1978, the Rainforest Alliance's SmartWood in 1989, and the Forest Stewardship Council (FSC) and Marine Stewardship Council (MSC) certification schemes in 1990 and 1997.

The proliferation of eco-labelling eventually led to the International Organisation

1967	First organic standard of the Soil Association (UK)
1978	Germany launches the Blue Angel eco-label
1988	Max Havelaar Foundation launches world's first fairtrade coffee
1988	*The Green Consumer Guide* published
1989	Rainforest Alliance launches SmartWood certification
1991	The Body Shop launches its Trade Not Aid initiative
1997	International Fairtrade Mark launched
1998	ISO 14020 on environmental labelling launched
1998	Ethical Trading Initiative established
2006	Wal-Mart commits to MSC fish stocks and organic cotton

for Standardisation (ISO) issuing ISO 14020 in 1998, the first in its suite of guidelines on environmental labelling, which includes ISO 14021, 14024 and 14025. Fuelling the increasing demand for eco-labels was the phenomenon of environmentally conscious shopping, as typified by *The Green Consumer Guide*, published in 1988 and said to have sold over a million copies.

At the same time, social issues were also on the rise. In 1988, the Dutch-based Max Havelaar Foundation launched the world's first fairtrade label, focused on improving the wages and working conditions of coffee farmers in Mexico. By 1997, social labelling had matured sufficiently to demand the introduction of an International Fairtrade Mark, which now applies to a growing diversity of globally sourced products, from tourism and wine to footballs and chocolate.

Ethical consumerism undoubtedly started as a fringe movement with marginal market impact. However, today, thanks at least in part to many of the world's largest companies such as Wal-Mart, Toyota, Unilever and GE coming on board, it is going mainstream. Fairtrade coffee now competes strongly with other top brands, carbon labelling is about to take off, and green-tech is one of the fastest-growing investment sectors.

Eco-labelling

The OECD defines environmental labelling as the 'voluntary granting of labels by a private or public body in order to inform consumers and thereby promote consumer products which are determined to be environmentally more friendly than other functionally and competitively similar products'.

The International Organisation for Standardisation (ISO) identifies three broad types of voluntary labels, with eco-labelling fitting under the Type I designation. Type I labels are a voluntary, multiple-criteria-based, third-party programme which awards a licence that authorises the use of environmental labels on products, indicating overall environmental preferability of a product within a particular product category based on life-cycle considerations (e.g. MSC, Soil Association certified).

The ISO standards on environmental labels and declarations are: ISO 14020:2000, ISO 14021:1999, ISO 14024:1999 and ISO 14025:2006.

Carbon labelling is a subset of eco-labelling. According to the Carbon Trust, a carbon label is a public measure of a product's carbon footprint from source to store, with a commitment from the business to reduce this figure.

The Global Ecolabelling Network is a non-profit association of third-party environmental performance labelling organisations founded in 1994 to improve, promote and develop the eco-labelling of products and services.

FACTBOX

- The world's first eco-label was launched by the Soil Association in the UK in 1967, followed by Germany's Blue Angel label in 1978.
- The most popular eco-labels in the world include: Dolphin-safe, MSC (Marine Stewardship Council), FSC (Forest Stewardship Council), Soil Association, USDA Organic, Bio (in Europe), EU Energy Label (on white goods) and Fairtrade.
- World organic food sales jumped from US$23 billion in 2002 to $40 billion in 2006. Organic farming is now practised in over 100 countries throughout the world, with more than 24 million hectares under organic management by 2004. Latin America leads, followed by Europe and North America.
- Over the past 13 years, over 90 million hectares in more than 70 countries have been certified according to FSC standards, and as of September 2007 there are 857 MSC-labelled seafood products sold in 34 countries worldwide.
- Tesco (the world's third largest retailer) is developing a carbon label and in the interim has put an aeroplane symbol on all air-freighted products. The Carbon Trust has already launched a carbon reduction label in the UK to provide a measure of a product's carbon footprint (embodied GHG emissions) across its life-cycle.

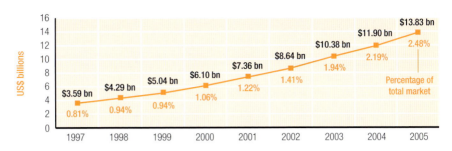

Figure 22 **Growth in US organic food sales (1997–2005)**
Source: Organic Trade Association

Fairtrade

Fairtade tries to ensure fairer working conditions and commodity prices for producers in developing countries, through a system of organisations, standards, product labels and independent auditing requirements.

However, fairtrade is not without its critics. Some argue that fairtrade (or ethical trade) often fails to involve or even recognise important social groups and omits many of the priority issues for communities and workers. They concede that this is not the result of technical failings in standards, auditing or stakeholder engagement but rather reflects the intrinsic nature of such instruments which reproduce culturally specific values.

FINE is an umbrella network that involves Fairtrade Labelling Organisations International (FLO), the World Fair Trade Organisation (IFAT), the Network of European Worldshops (NEWS!) and the European Fair Trade Association (EFTA).

FINE defines fairtrade as a trading partnership, based on dialogue, transparency and respect, that seeks greater equity in international trade. It contributes to sustainable development by offering better trading conditions to, and securing the rights of, marginalised producers and workers especially in the South.

FLO is the leading fairtrade standard-setting and certification body. Established in 1997 and located in Bonn, Germany, it is the umbrella organisation for a worldwide network of fairtrade organisations. FLO members currently operate in 15 European countries as well as Australia, Canada, Japan, Mexico, New Zealand and the United States.

The Fairtrade Mark is a label carried on a product as a consumer guarantee that it meets the fairtrade standards set and verified by the FLO. These producer and trader standards provide guarantees of better prices and conditions to the producers growing or making them.

astings, UK,
erman with the
ine Stewardship
ncil logo

FACTBOX

- From the introduction of the first fairtrade coffee in the Netherlands in 1988 and the establishment of the Fairtrade Foundation in Britain in 1992, fairtrade has spread to become an international movement covering 22 consumer countries and over 60 producer countries.
- In 2006, there were over 2000 fairtrade-certified products in the UK alone.
- Market penetration of fairtrade products in some markets is also becoming significant — with, for example, over 20% of UK roast and ground coffee sales.
- Big international brands that have embraced fairtrade products include Tesco (the third largest retail group in the world) and Starbucks.

A fairtrade coffee farmer
istockphoto

BOOKS

John Elkington and Julia Hailes, *The Green Consumer Guide. From Shampoo to Champagne: High Street Shopping for a Better Environment* (Gollancz, 1988)

Fair Trade Advocacy Office, *Business Unusual: Successes and Challenges of Fair Trade* (Fair Trade Advocacy Office, 2006)

Julia Hailes, *The New Green Consumer Guide* (Simon & Schuster, 2007)

Harriet Lamb, *Fighting the Banana Wars and Other Fairtrade Battles: How We Took on the Corporate Giants to Change the World* (Rider & Co., 2008)

Charlotte Mulvey, *The Good Shopping Guide: Revealing the Good, the Bad and the Ugly of Ethical Shopping Brands* (Ethical Marketing Group, 6th rev. edn, 2007)

Alex Nicholls and Charlotte Opal, *Fair Trade: Market-Driven Ethical Consumption* (Sage Publications, 2005)

Bruce Phillips, Trevor Ward and Chet Chaffee, *Eco-labelling in Fisheries: What Is It All About?* (Blackwell, 2003)

Thomas Princen, Michael Maniates and Ken Conca (eds.), *Confronting Consumption* (MIT Press, 2002)

Frieder Rubik and Paolo Frankl (eds.), *The Future of Eco-labelling: Making Environmental Product Information Systems Effective* (Greenleaf Publishing, 2005)

Joseph Stiglitz and Andrew Charlton, *Fair Trade for All: How Trade Can Promote Development* (OUP, 2005)

REPORTS

I Will If You Will: Towards Sustainable Consumption (UK Sustainable Consumption Roundtable, 2006)

Sustainable Consumption and Production: A Business Primer (University of Cambridge Programme for Sustainability Leadership.

Based on a report produced by the UK Government's Business Taskforce on Sustainable Consumption and Production, 2007)

What Assures Consumers? (AccountAbility and the National Consumer Council [NCC], 2006)

WEBSITES

Business Taskforce on Sustainable Consumption and Production: www.cpi.cam.ac.uk/programmes/ sustainable_consumption/scp_taskforce. aspx

Ethical Consumer: www.ethicalconsumer.org

Ethical Trading Initiative (ETI): www.ethicaltrade.org

European Fair Trade Association (EFTA): www.european-fair-trade-association.org

Fair Labor Association: www.fairlabor.org

Fairtrade Foundation (UK): www.fairtrade.org.uk

Fairtrade Labelling Organisations International (FLO): www.fairtrade.net

Global Ecolabelling Network: www.globalecolabelling.net

IFAT: The World Fair Trade Organisation: www.ifat.org

International Organic Accreditation Service: www.ioas.org

International Social and Environmental Accreditation and Labelling (ISEAL) Alliance: www.isealalliance.org

UNEP Sustainable Consumption website: www.unep.org/themes/consumption/index. asp

UK Sustainable Consumption Roundtable (SCR): www.sd-commission.org.uk/pages/ consumption.html

MANAGEMENT

V

17

CODES AND STANDARDS

Can it be good governance to comply mindlessly with the guidelines in a code? In a 'comply or else' regime, one finds a quantitative tick-box approach rather than an application of mind to process.

MERVYN KING, Chairman, Global Reporting Initiative and King Committee on Corporate Governance in South Africa

In corporate responsibility, there is a continuum from values, through principles and codes, to norms and standards. Standards apply broadly and entail a greater degree of accountability and consensus among stakeholders.

DEBORAH LEIPZIGER, author and consultant in corporate social responsibility (CSR)

What we are witnessing is a shift from static notions of accountability as a function of compliance with institutional norms, standards and laws to a more dynamic understanding — in effect, a social contract that is being constantly rewritten.

MARIA SILLANPÄÄ, Director, Sustainability Advisory Group

An effective management system is central to avoidance of environmental degradation and provides a framework for a clear and focused approach to environmental improvement.

RICHARD WELFORD, author on environmental management and co-founder of CSR Asia

Child labour in
Philippi
Jon Fabr

Institutionalising continuous improvement...

The story of certification can be traced back to 1982 with the work of the so-called father of the modern quality movement, W. Edwards Deming. His quality management cycle of Plan–Do–Check–Review underpins the International Organisation for Standardisation's ISO 9000 standards and also became the backbone of the ISO 14001 approach to continuous improvement in environmental management. With ISO 9001 and ISO 9002 already widely used around the world, ISO 14001 was quickly adopted and became the second most popular certifiable standard.

While ISO 14001 built on the ISO 9000 process approach, it looked for content guidance to the Eco-Management and Audit (EMAS) scheme, enacted by the European parliament in 1993. The standards are similar, with the notable difference that EMAS includes a requirement for annual public reporting. This disclosure clause anticipated the trend towards sustainability (or non-financial) reporting, which had grown to 64% among Global *Fortune* 250 companies by 2005, according to a KPMG survey.

Reflecting and stimulating this growing trend, the Global Reporting Initiative, established in 1997, launched its Sustainability Reporting Guidelines in 2000, with a vision to make non-financial reporting as commonplace and comparable as financial reporting. Although the Guidelines are not a certifiable standard, organisations are encouraged to make a public declaration about their compliance.

Two significant standards emerged in 1997. The launch of SA8000 was a US response to the growing emphasis on (and criticism of) labour conditions in multinational supply chains. The launch coincided with a high-profile exposé of poor working conditions in the factory of one of Nike's suppliers in Vietnam. In a complementary development, the launch of the international Fairtrade label signalled the maturation of the European-led fairtrade movement, which mainly focused on the plight of small-scale farmers.

Two years later, in 1999, AccountAbility launched its AA1000 Framework standard as guidance on stakeholder engagement, linked into the measurement and reporting cycle. The same year saw the British Standards Institution release its OHSAS 18001 management system standard for occupational health and safety, making it compatible with ISO 9000 and ISO 14001.

There is currently no indication that ISO will develop its own health and safety standard. However, it is very active in two other emerging areas. The first is greenhouse gas management — with ISO 14064 launched in 2006 and ISO 14065 in 2007: a response to the explosion of interest and urgency around climate change. And the second is social responsibility, with the guidance standard ISO 26000 due for release in 2010.

This trend of standardisation and performance verification will doubtless continue, although it is likely we will see an increasing emphasis on compatibility with existing standards, and issue- and sector-specific responses.

1987 ISO 9000 standards on quality management published

1993 Eco-Management and Audit Scheme (EMAS) enacted by the EU

1996 ISO 14001 environmental management standard launched

1997 SA8000 standard on social accountability published

1997 Fairtrade standard launched internationally

1999 AA1000 Framework standard on accountability published

1999 OHSAS 18001 standard on occupational health and safety published

2000 GRI Sustainability Reporting Guidelines launched

2000 UN Global Compact principles launched

2006 ISO 14064 standard on GHG accounting and verification launched

ISO 14001

ISO 14001 is an environmental management systems (EMS) standard issued by the International Organisation for Standardisation (ISO) in 1996, and revised in 2004.

ISO 14001:2004 defines an environmental management system as that part of the overall management system of an organisation that includes organisational structure, planning activities, responsibilities, practices, procedures, processes and resources for developing, implementing, achieving, reviewing and maintaining an environmental policy.

ISO 14001 is part of the ISO 14000 series of standards and guideline reference documents, which fall under the ISO Technical Committee 207 and cover the following:

- Environmental Management Systems: 14001, 14004
- Environmental Auditing and Related Environmental Investigations: 14015
- Environmental Labelling: 14020, 14021, 14024, 14025
- Environmental Performance Evaluation: 14031, 14032
- Life Cycle Assessment: 14040, 14044, 14047, 14048, 14049
- Greenhouse Gas Management and Related Activities: 14064, 14065

ISO 14001 is the only certification standard in the series, and requires auditing by an accredited independent third party.

One of the great strengths of ISO 14001 is that it was designed to be compatible with the ISO 9000 series on quality management and embraces the principle of continuous improvement.

OHSAS 18001 (a non-ISO standard by BSI) has followed this principle and developed an occupational health and safety standard to be compatible with ISO 14001.

Although ISO 14001 remains the most popular environmental management systems standard, many argue that the EU Eco-Management and Audit Scheme (EMAS) established in 1993 is a more comprehensive standard, since it includes the requirement to produce an annual public report on environmental performance.

FACTBOX

▶ To date, there have been around 130,000 ISO 14001 certifications worldwide in 138 countries.

▶ An estimated 20 million people worldwide work in ISO 14001-certified organisations.

▶ The top ten countries for ISO 14001 growth include: Japan, China, Korea, Italy, Spain, the Czech Republic, France, Turkey, India and Romania.

▶ The top five industrial sectors with ISO 14001 certification include: electrical and optical equipment; basic metal and fabricated metal products; construction; wholesale and retail trade; and chemicals, chemical products and fibres.

▶ Certification is not limited to industrial activity. Major banks and some NGOs (e.g. Forum for the Future, WWF) have sought certification.

▶ The challenge remains to get more SMEs (small and medium-sized enterprises) and suppliers ISO 14001-certified — though ISO prides itself on the fact that more than 200 German chimney sweepers are certified to the standard.

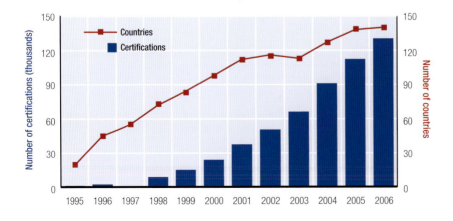

Figure 23 **Number of ISO 14001 certifications and country representation**
Source: ISO

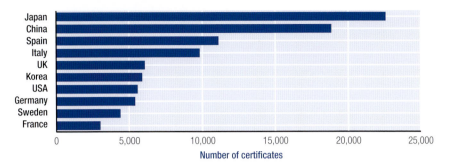

Figure 24 **Top 10 countries for ISO 14001 certification**
Source: ISO

Spotlight: SA8000

In 1997, Social Accountability International (SAI) was established and convened an expert international, multi-stakeholder advisory board to partner in developing standards and systems to address workers' rights.

Published in late 1997 and revised in 2001, the SA8000 standard is an auditable certification standard based on international workplace norms of the International Labour Organisation (ILO) conventions, the Universal Declaration of Human Rights and the UN Convention on the Rights of the Child.

In addition to clauses on discrimination, health and safety, freedom of association, collective bargaining, compensation and management systems, the SA8000 system has the following specific requirements:

- Child labour: no workers under the age of 15; minimum lowered to 14 for countries operating under the ILO Convention 138 developing-country exception; remediation of any child found to be working;

- Forced labour: no forced labour, including prison or debt bondage labour; no lodging of deposits or identity papers by employers or outside recruiters;

- Discipline: no corporal punishment, mental or physical coercion or verbal abuse; and

- Working hours: comply with the applicable law but, in any event, no more than 48 hours per week with at least one day off for every seven-day period; voluntary overtime paid at a premium rate and not to exceed 12 hours per week on a regular basis; exceptions for regular and overtime limits due to extraordinary circumstances.

The standard is subject to independent, expert verification of compliance by SAI-accredited certification bodies. In addition, certified facilities are required to report publicly on their progress.

FACTBOX

▶ There are over 1,460 facilities certified to SA8000 in 65 countries covering 67 industries.

▶ Retailers, brand companies and other employers worldwide — with 675,000 employees and annual sales over US$175 billion — are using SA8000.

▶ According to the International Labour Organisation (ILO), there are an estimated 218 million child labourers worldwide. Of these, 126 million are in hazardous work. While the incidence of children's work is highest in sub-Saharan Africa, the largest number of child workers can be found in the Asia-Pacific region.

▶ The ILO further estimates that 12.3 million people are victims of forced labour (9.8 million exploited by private agents and 2.5 million forced to work by the state or by rebel military groups), while more than 2.4 million have been trafficked. Of these, 9.5 million are from the Asia and Pacific region.

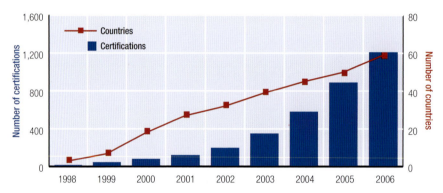

Figure 25 **Number of SA8000 certifications and country representation**
Source: Social Accountability International

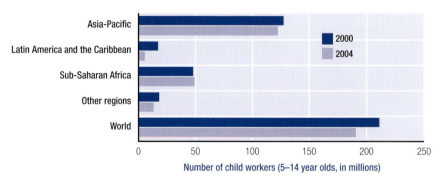

Figure 26 **Child labour 2000–2004**
Source: International Labour Organisation (ILO)

BOOKS

Wayne Visser, Dirk Matten, Manfred Pohl and Nick Tolhurst (eds.), *The A to Z of Corporate Social Responsibility: The Complete Reference of Concepts, Codes and Organisations* (John Wiley, 2007)

Rhys Jenkins, Ruth Pearson and Gill Seyfang, *Corporate Responsibility and Labour Rights: Codes of Conduct in the Global Economy* (Earthscan, 2002)

Deborah Leipziger, *The Corporate Responsibility Code Book* (Greenleaf Publishing, 2003)

Richard Welford and Andrew Gouldson, *Environmental Management and Business Strategy* (Financial Times/Prentice Hall, 1993)

Stefan Schaltegger, Roger Burritt and Holger Petersen, *An Introduction to Corporate Environmental Management: Striving for Sustainability* (Greenleaf Publishing, 2003)

Christopher Sheldon (ed.), *ISO 14001 and Beyond: Environmental Management Systems in the Real World* (Greenleaf Publishing, 1997)

Ruth Hillary (ed.), *ISO 14001: Case Studies and Practical Experiences* (Greenleaf Publishing, 2000)

Marc J. Epstein, *Making Sustainability Work: Best Practices in Managing and Measuring Corporate Social, Environmental, and Economic Impacts* (Greenleaf Publishing/Berrett-Koehler, 2008)

Jan Jonker and Marco de Witte (eds.), *Management Models for Corporate Social Responsibility* (Springer, 2006)

Robert Sroufe and Joseph Sarkis (eds.), *Strategic Sustainability: The State of the Art in Corporate Environmental Management Systems* (Greenleaf Publishing, 2007)

REPORTS

ISO 14001:2004 — Environmental Management Systems — Requirements with Guidance for Use (International Organisation for Standardisation, 2004)

SA8000 (Social Accountability International, 2001)

Sustainability Reporting Guidelines: Version 3.0 (Global Reporting Initiative, 2006)

WEBSITES

AccountAbility: www.accountability21.net

EU Eco-Management and Audit Scheme (EMAS): ec.europa.eu/environment/emas

Fairtrade Labelling Organisations International (FLO): www.fairtrade.net

Global Reporting Initiative (GRI): www.globalreporting.org

International Organisation for Standardisation: ISO 9000 and ISO 14000: www.iso.org/iso/iso_catalogue/management_standards/iso_9000_iso_14000.htm

Social Accountability International: www.sa-intl.org

Sustainable Integrated Guidelines for Management (SIGMA) Project: www.projectsigma.co.uk

18

CORPORATE GOVERNANCE

The culture of greed at Enron corrupted everybody and everything that came into contact with it.

DICK DEGUERIN, attorney in the Enron case

Whenever an institution malfunctions as consistently as boards of directors have in nearly every major fiasco of the last forty or fifty years it is futile to blame men. It is the institution that malfunctions.

PETER DRUCKER, management author

Corporate governance is concerned with holding the balance between economic and social goals and between individual and communal goals. The governance framework encourages the efficient use of resources and requires accountability for the stewardship of those resources.

SIR ADRIAN CADBURY, former Chairman of Cadbury Schweppes, **Director of the Bank of England and Chairman of the UK Committee on the Financial Aspects of Corporate Governance**

If a few rotten apples can spoil the barrel, I think we have to look at the nature of the barrel, not just the apples.

ROSABETH MOSS KANTER, management author
and former editor of *Harvard Business Review*

Enron's 'Cod
Eth
Mark B

|Code|of Ethics

July, 2000

Ensuring accountability to shareholders and stakeholders...

Although corporate governance dates back to the 19th century, when the rights of corporate boards to manage on behalf of shareholders were enhanced, the modern corporate governance era really began with the creation of the Committee on the Financial Aspects of Corporate Governance by the UK's Financial Reporting Council, London Stock Exchange and accounting profession in 1991.

The Committee was chaired by Sir Adrian Cadbury, then Director of the Bank of England and retired Chairman of Cadbury Schweppes. It issued its findings in 1992 in a report entitled *Financial Aspects of Corporate Governance*, more popularly known as the Cadbury Report. The report, including its code of best practice, became a benchmark for corporate governance initiatives around the world.

One of the countries to pursue this guidance most actively was South Africa, which set up the King Committee on Corporate Governance in 1993, under the auspices of the Institute of Directors in Southern Africa and chaired by former South African High Court judge, Mervyn E. King. Its first report, issued in 1994, broke new ground by specifically incorporating recommendations on codes of ethics and stakeholder consultation.

Meanwhile, the UK continued to build its corporate governance framework, with the 1995 Greenbury Report making recommendations on the remuneration of directors, which was combined with Cad-

bury to form the Combined Code in 1998. Furthermore, in 1999, the Turnbull Report provided guidance on systems of internal control, and Principles and Guidelines on Corporate Governance were launched by the OECD and Commonwealth respectively.

In 2001, the Enron scandal broke in the United States, with evidence of financial irregularities sending its stocks into freefall. In the space of ten months, the company filed for bankruptcy, taking its accountants, Arthur Andersen, down with it. Another accounting scandal involving more than $3 billion at WorldCom followed shortly thereafter, resulting in the telephone company's demise in 2002.

According to *Forbes* magazine, there were 22 accounting scandals in the US between June 2000 and September 2002. However, Europe was not immune. In 2003, dairy-foods giant Parmalat was investigated for fabricating assets to offset over US$16 billion in debt and liabilities over a 15-year period, leading to its bankruptcy. Meanwhile, the global retailer Ahold was found to have overstated its earnings position by $880 million.

In the US, the response was the Sarbanes–Oxley Act of 2002, which strengthened accounting controls and disclosure requirements. In South Africa, the King Report was updated, notably improving sections on risk management and business ethics, while introducing a new chapter on Integrated Sustainability Reporting. In the UK, the Combined Code was also updated, incorporating in 2003 the recommendations from reports on the role of non-executive directors (the Higgs Report) and the role of the audit committee (the Smith Report). Despite the danger of encouraging a 'tick-box' compliance mentality, these codes and legal requirements appear to have been fairly effective, at least for the time being.

1992	Cadbury Report issued in the UK
1994	King Report issued in South Africa (revised in 2002)
1998	Combined Code issued in the UK (updated in 2003 and 2006)
1999	OECD Principles of Corporate Governance launched (revised in 2004)
1999	Commonwealth Association of Corporate Governance (CACG) Guidelines issued
2001	Enron files for bankruptcy in the US
2002	WorldCom files for bankruptcy in the US
2002	Arthur Andersen surrenders its CPA licence and goes out of business
2002	Sarbanes–Oxley Act promulgated in the US
2003	Parmalat financial scandal in Europe

Former Enron Chairman Kenneth Lay (left) and former Enron CEO Jeff Skilling at Enron Headquarters
Wyatt McSpadden

Enron collapse

Enron, formed in 1931, grew into one of the world's leading electricity, natural gas, pulp and paper, and communications companies.

Enron was named 'America's Most Innovative Company' by *Fortune* magazine for six consecutive years, from 1996 to 2001, and was on *Fortune's* '100 Best Companies to Work for in America' list in 2000. It was also seen as a leader in corporate social responsibility (CSR).

When financial irregularities were discovered in August 2001, the stock price plummeted and, by December, Enron filed for bankruptcy.

Enron used an accounting technique called 'mark to market', which allowed it to mark future earnings at today's prices. In addition, it used 'related-party transactions' (i.e. businesses set up and controlled by Enron to whom they 'sold' services) to generate artificial revenues.

Arthur Andersen, Enron's accountants and at the time one of the top five accounting firms in the world, was implicated in the scandal, having shredded key documents, and collapsed in 2002.

Spoof Enron logo

FACTBOX

- In 2000, Enron had revenues of $111 billion and employed over 20,000 staff.
- Enron's stock price dropped from $90 to just a few cents in the space of ten months in 2001.
- The average severance payment was $45,000, while executives received bonuses of $55 million in the company's last year.
- Employees lost $1.2 billion in pensions; retirees lost $2 billion; while executives cashed in $116 million in stocks.
- The dissolution of Andersen resulted in the loss of 85,000 jobs around the world.
- Jeffrey K. Skilling, the former chief executive of Enron, pleaded not guilty but was found guilty on 19 counts of fraud, conspiracy, insider trading and lying to auditors. He was sentenced to more than 24 years in prison and a fine of $45 million.
- Andrew S. Fastow, the former chief financial officer, was sentenced in September 2006 to six years in prison.
- Kenneth L. Lay, Enron's founder and chairman, was found guilty on ten counts, but died of heart problems before sentence was passed.
- After a six-year class action lawsuit by 1.5 million Enron shareholders who bought shares between 1997 and 2001, a settlement was reached whereby investors will receive $6.79 per share (despite many having paid up to $90 per share).
- The settlement will be paid for by a $7.2 billion compensation fund that was set up following class action lawsuits against the banks that did business with Enron, which shareholders allege were aiding and abetting fraud.

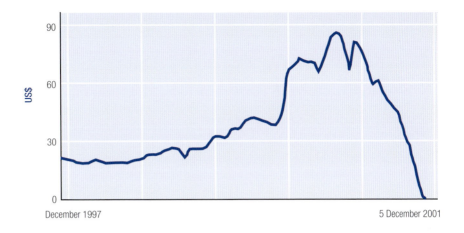

Figure 27 **Enron stock price collapse**
Source: *Business Week*/Bloomberg Financial Markets

King Report on Corporate Governance

Following the example of the UK's Committee on the Financial Aspects of Corporate Governance, chaired by Sir Adrian Cadbury, the Institute of Directors in Southern Africa (IODSA) established the King Committee on Corporate Governance in July 1993.

The King Committee was named after its Chair, former South African High Court judge and corporate lawyer and current Chairman of the Global Reporting Initiative, Mervyn E. King.

The first King Report on Corporate Governance was published in November 1994 and was distinguished by its embracing of an inclusive approach to corporate governance.

In particular, it incorporated requirements for a code of corporate practices and conduct that looked beyond the corporation itself, and was the first corporate governance report to specifically refer to stakeholders. In so doing it went beyond the purely financial focus of the Cadbury Report in the UK.

In 2002, the IODSA launched a revision of the King Report ('King II'), which included an entire chapter on Integrated Sustainability Reporting, heavily referencing the Global Reporting Initiative's Sustainability Reporting Guidelines and AccountAbility's AA1000 standard.

FACTBOX

▶ In 2003, KPMG surveyed the top 100 companies listed on the JSE Securities Exchange SA to determine the level of compliance with the sustainability reporting requirements of King II and found that:

- Eighty-five per cent of companies surveyed provided annual reporting on sustainability-related issues and 77% of the companies referenced the existence of an internal code of ethics or code of corporate conduct.

- The most frequently disclosed issues included: health and safety (including HIV/AIDS), employment equity, and social investment (including black economic empowerment).

- While many JSE-listed companies were incorporating sustainability disclosures in their annual reports, 20% also produced a stand-alone non-financial report. This number had increased from 16% in 2002. An additional 6% of companies indicated that they intend to produce a non-financial report for the current financial year.

The reporting trend stimulated by King II appears to have sustained momentum, with KPMG's 2006 comparative survey finding increased reporting on employment equity (up to 82% from 79%), corporate social investment (up to 86% from 72%), HIV/AIDS (up to 73% from 67%), health and safety (up to 77% from 59%) and environmental management (up to 70% from 55%).

In addition, King II was one of the catalysts for establishing the Johannesburg Securities Exchange (JSE)'s Socially Responsible Investment (SRI) Index, launched in May 2004 and the first of its kind in an emerging market.

Topics most frequently disclosed in 2006 as a percentage of survey sample

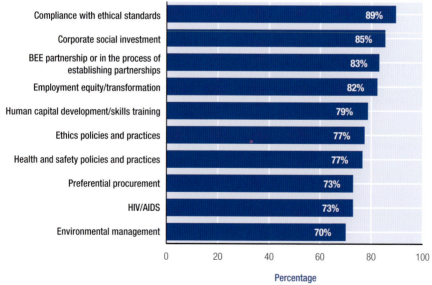

BEE = Black Economic Empowerment

Figure 28 **Sustainability reporting by JSE-listed companies in South Africa (2006)**
Source: KPMG, *2006 Survey of Integrated Sustainability Reporting in South Africa*

BOOKS

Adrian Cadbury, *Corporate Governance and Chairmanship: A Personal View* (OUP, 2002)

Istemi Demirag (ed.), *Corporate Social Responsibility, Accountability and Governance: Global Perspectives* (Greenleaf Publishing, 2005)

Lynne W. Jeter, *Disconnected: Deceit and Betrayal at WorldCom* (John Wiley, 2003)

Bethany McLean and Peter Elkind, *The Smartest Guys in the Room: The Amazing Rise and Scandalous Fall of Enron* (Viking, 2003)

Peter C. Fusaro and Ross M. Miller, *What Went Wrong at Enron: Everyone's Guide to the Largest Bankruptcy in US History* (John Wiley, 2002)

Barbara Ley Toffler and Jennifer Reingold, *Final Accounting: Ambition, Greed, and the Fall of Arthur Andersen* (Broadway Books, 2003)

REPORTS

CACG Guidelines: Principles for Corporate Governance in the Commonwealth (Commonwealth Association of Corporate Governance [CACG], 1999)

Combined Code: Principles of Good Governance and Code of Best Practice (UK Committee on Corporate Governance, 2003)

Corporate Governance (Mervyn E. King; in Wayne Visser, Dirk Matten, Manfred Pohl and Nick Tolhurst [eds.], *The A to Z of Corporate Social Responsibility: The Complete Reference of Concepts, Codes and Organisations* [John Wiley, 2007])

Financial Aspects of Corporate Governance (Cadbury Report) (Committee on the Financial Aspects of Corporate Governance, 1992)

King Report on Corporate Governance in South Africa (Institute of Directors in Southern Africa, 2002)

WEBSITES

European Corporate Governance Institute: www.ecgi.org

Financial Reporting Council (UK): www.frc.org.uk

Global Reporting Initiative (GRI): www.globalreporting.org

Institute of Directors in Southern Africa (IoD): www.iodsa.co.za

International Corporate Governance Network (ICGN): www.icgn.org

Sarbanes–Oxley Act: www.sarbanes-oxley.com

19

SUSTAINABILITY REPORTING

Non-financial reporting should improve performance, provided that information recipients have some sort of power in the relationship with corporate or organizational management. Maybe that aspect of this debate has not been played out fully yet... how do non-shareholder stakeholders exert power and how can they use public reporting tools to enable them to do that?

ROGER ADAMS, **Executive Director, Association of Chartered Certified Accountants (ACCA)**

We don't think you can really even understand performance — measure it, benchmark it, or reward it — unless you first have this underlying level of disclosure that allows external stakeholders to judge whether or not a company is performing.

BROOKE BARTON, **Manager of Corporate Accountability Programs at Ceres**

Definition of 'greenwash': You can't put a lettuce in the window of a butcher's shop and declare that you are now 'turning vegetarian'.

JOHN GRANT, **author of *The Green Marketing Manifesto***

Companies that do not transparently communicate their sustainability performance are running out of excuses.

SIR MARK MOODY STUART, **Chairman of Anglo American plc and member of the GRI Board of Directors**

What gets measured gets managed . . .

The trend of sustainability reporting is largely a phenomenon of the past 15 years. Prior to this, disclosure by companies on their social and environmental performance tended to focus on philanthropic projects and health and safety statistics in their annual financial reports, or glossy public relations brochures and reports of community involvement.

This began to change as activist groups criticised companies for their poor environmental performance and lack of transparency. Meanwhile, industry initiatives such as Responsible Care started to systematise the collection of data, and emerging corporate governance codes such as the King Report encouraged public reporting.

Soon, environmental management system standards, such as the 1993 EU Eco-Management and Audit Scheme, required the publication of a public statement of performance, and some countries made environmental reporting com-

1993 EMAS (Eco-Management and Audit Scheme) includes environmental reporting requirements

1993 UNEP (UN Environment Programme) and SustainAbility issue their environmental reporting study

1993 KPMG launches international survey of environmental reporting

1994 London Benchmarking Group established

1995 WICE (World Industry Council on the Environment) publishes guidelines for voluntary environmental reporting

1998 UNCTAD (UN Conference on Trade and Development) issues environmental accounting and reporting guidelines

1998 WRI (World Resources Institute)/WBCSD (World Business Council for Sustainable Development) Greenhouse Gas Protocol launched

2000 GRI (Global Reporting Initiative) Sustainability Reporting Guidelines launched

2000 Carbon Disclosure Project established

2003 AA1000 Assurance Standard launched

pulsory for certain sectors and sizes of companies.

The accounting and consulting sector spotted the trend, with companies such as KPMG and SustainAbility launching the first international surveys of environmental reporting in 1993. Others, including the Association of Chartered Certified Accountants (ACCA) and Business in the Community, then began to host reporting awards, while the London Benchmarking Group encouraged voluntary disclosure between companies.

The form of reporting closely mirrored the trend of integration happening in companies, first joining environment together with health and safety, then adding social/community dimensions, and finally adopting the triple bottom line of sustainability and CSR (corporate social responsibility) reporting.

This trend was consolidated when the Global Reporting Initiative (GRI) was initiated by Ceres in 1998 and issued its first Sustainability Reporting Guidelines in 1999. Revised in 2002 and 2006, the GRI Guidelines have become the framework for standardisation and benchmarking.

Meanwhile, with the rapid escalation of climate change as a critical issue, the need for reliable data led the World Resources Institute (WRI) and the World Business Council for Sustainable Development (WBCSD) to formulate the Greenhouse Gas Protocol in 1998 to provide a common platform for carbon emissions measurement and reporting. This was followed in 2000 by the creation of the Carbon Disclosure Project, which encourages improved reporting by the FT500 on behalf of institutional investors.

In parallel with the rise of sustainability and greenhouse gas reporting, there has been a concerted attempt to standardise third-party assurance or independent verification, leading to the development of accounting standards such as ISAE 3000 and more specific CSR/sustainability guidance such as the AA1000 Assurance Standard.

There is still a healthy discussion about the value and credibility of sustainability reporting, but the goal of generating comparable social, environmental and economic performance data draws ever closer.

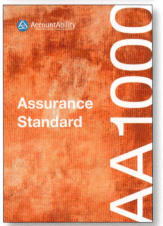

AccountAbility's
AA1000 Assurance
Standard
AccountAbility

SustainAbility's *2006
Survey of Corporate
Sustainability Reporting*
SustainAbility

Global Reporting Initiative (GRI)

The Global Reporting Initiative (GRI) began as a Ceres project in 1998, with the United Nations Environment Programme (UNEP) joining as a partner in 1999. It was incorporated as an independent non-profit organisation in 2002 with its head office in Amsterdam.

GRI's Sustainability Reporting Guidelines — first published in 1999, and revised in 2002 (G2) and 2006 (G3) — set out the principles and indicators that organisations can use to measure and report their economic, environmental and social performance.

The Guidelines act as a framework for the structure and content of sustainability reports, covering the following areas:

- Defining report content
- Defining report quality
- Setting the report boundary
- Profile disclosures
- Disclosure on management approach
- Performance indicators

There are 79 performance indicators including 49 core (compulsory) indicators. The indicators are grouped into 9 economic measures, 30 environmental measures and 40 social measures (including 14 labour, 9 human rights, 8 society and 9 product responsibility).

The Guidelines have Sector Supplements for: Financial Services; Logistics and Transportation; Mining and Metals; Public Agency; Tour Operators; Telecommunications; and Automotive. Special guidance is also available for small and medium-sized enterprises (SMEs) and HIV/AIDS reporting.

FACTBOX

- To date, more than 1,500 organisations have declared their voluntary adoption of the Guidelines worldwide.
- Over 16,000 CSR (corporate social responsibility)/sustainability reports across more than 4,200 companies have been included in the Corporate Registers database.
- According to research by KPMG, sustainability reporting has been steadily rising since 1993, from 45% of the Global Top 250 companies in 2002 to 79% in 2008.
- According to CorporateRegister, the number of CSR/sustainability reports has grown from 27 in 1992 to 2,500 in 2007. European companies have taken the lead and still produce over three times as many reports as the next most prolific regions — a tie between Asia and North and Central America.
- The focus has shifted from environmental reports in the early 1990s to health, safety and environment reports in the mid-1990s, to sustainability and CSR reports in the 2000s.
- In 2007, 29% of CSR/sustainability reports included an external verification statement, of which 10% used the AA1000 Assurance Standard.
- Over a million reports were accessed on CorporateRegister.com during 2008, primarily by students, people working in support services, consultants and corporate CSR/sustainability professionals.

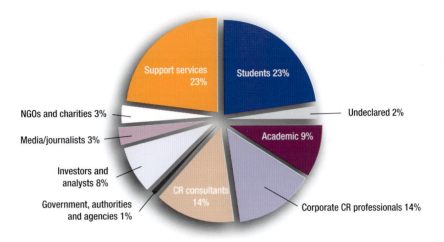

Figure 29 **Who's viewing the reports, by stakeholder group (November 2007–January 2008)**

Source: CorporateRegister.com, *CR Reporting Awards 07: Global Winners and Reporting Trends*, March 2008

Carbon Disclosure Project

The Carbon Disclosure Project (CDP) was established in 2000 to improve the response of companies to climate change, in particular by improving the quality and quantity of information on corporate climate impacts.

Today, CDP provides a coordinating secretariat for institutional investors with combined assets of over $57 trillion under management. On their behalf it seeks information on the business risks and opportunities presented by climate change and greenhouse gas emissions data from the world's largest companies: these numbered 3,000 in 2008.

Although completion of the annual climate change questionnaire is voluntary, because CDP acts on behalf of institutional investors, companies are more inclined to participate.

In order to ensure consistency of data reported, companies are encouraged to report their emissions data according to the Greenhouse Gas (GHG) Protocol, developed by the World Resources Institute (WRI) and the World Business Council for Sustainable Development (WBCSD) in 1998.

Over eight years CDP has become the gold standard for carbon disclosure methodology and process. The CDP website is the largest repository of corporate greenhouse gas emissions data in the world.

FACTBOX

► 77% (383) of the FT500 answered the CDP questionnaire in 2007, with total greenhouse gas (GHG) emissions reported of nearly 7 billion tonnes of CO_2e (carbon dioxide equivalent). Around a third of emissions were from fuel combustion, manufacturing activities and the generation of electricity purchased off the grid.

► 82% of responding companies considered climate change to present commercial opportunities for both existing and new products and services, while 79% thought it presented commercial risks.

► Of the companies that saw it as a commercial risk, 95% have implemented a GHG reduction programme with a specific target and timeline, compared to 76% overall (up from 48% in 2006).

► 34% of responding companies reported purchasing a percentage of their energy from renewable sources. In 2006, global investment in sustainable energy reached US$70.9 billion.

► 64% of responding carbon-intensive companies have allocated board-level or upper-management responsibility for climate change.

► Approximately 1.6 billion tonnes of CO_2e, worth US$29 billion, were traded in 2006.

► According to CorporateRegister.com in 2007, of the two-thirds of the Global FT500 that issued a stand-alone non-financial (CSR/sustainability) report, 87% address climate change and 78% publish greenhouse gas emissions data.

► 44% of Global FT500 CSR/sustainability reporters provide external assurance (independent verification) with their climate change disclosures. In Europe, three in five European reporters include verification, compared with one in ten for North American companies.

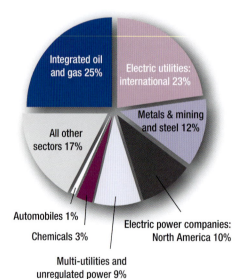

Figure 30 **Breakdown of 2006 direct and electricity emissions by sector**

Source: Innovest Strategic Value Advisors, *Carbon Disclosure Project Report 2007: Global FT500*

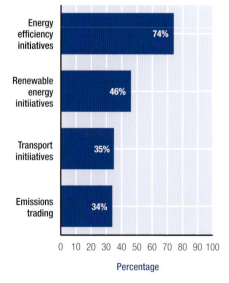

Figure 31 **Mitigation measures referenced**

Source: CorporateRegister.com, *The Corporate Climate Communications Report 2007* (February 2008)

BOOKS

Rob Gray, Dave Owen and Carol Adams, *Accounting and Accountability: Changes and Challenges in Corporate Social and Environmental Reporting* (Financial Times/ Prentice Hall, 1996)

Martin Bennett and Peter James (eds.), *Sustainable Measures: Evaluation and Reporting of Environmental and Social Performance* (Greenleaf Publishing, 1999)

Stefan Schaltegger, Martin Bennett and Roger Burritt (eds.), *Sustainability Accounting and Reporting* (Springer, 2006)

REPORTS

AA1000 Assurance Standard (AccountAbility, 2003)

Biodiversity Resource Document (Global Reporting Initiative [GRI], 2007)

Carbon Disclosure Project Report 2007: Global FT500

Communicating Business Contributions on the Millennium Development Goals (Global Reporting Initiative [GRI], 2004)

The Corporate Climate Communications Report 2007: A Study of Climate Change Disclosures by the Global FT500 (CorporateRegister.com, 2008)

Corporate Responsibility Reports: The Role of Assurance Providers and Stakeholder Panels (PricewaterhouseCoopers [PwC], 2008)

CR Reporting Awards 07 Official Report: Global Winners and Reporting Trends (CorporateRegister.com, 2008)

A Director's Guide to Corporate Responsibility Reporting (Business in the Community, 2005)

KPMG International Survey of Corporate Responsibility Reporting 2008 (KPMG)

Past, Present, Future: All You Need to Know About the G3 Guidelines (Global Reporting Initiative [GRI], 2007)

Reporting the Business Implications of Climate Change in Sustainability Reports (Global Reporting Initiative [GRI] and KPMG, 2008)

Tomorrow's Value: The Global Reporters 2006 Survey of Corporate Sustainability Reporting (SustainAbility, Standard & Poor's and United Nations Environment Programme [UNEP])

WEBSITES

ACCA sustainability webpage: www.accaglobal.com/sustainability

AccountAbility: www.accountability21.net

Business in the Community: www.bitc.org.uk

Carbon Disclosure Project: www.cdproject.net

CorporateRegister.com: www.corporateregister.com

EU Eco-Management and Audit Scheme (EMAS): ec.europa.eu/environment/emas

Global Reporting Initiative (GRI): www.globalreporting.org

Greenhouse Gas Protocol: www.ghgprotocol.org

International Corporate Sustainability Reporting Site: www.enviroreporting.com

KPMG Sustainability webpage: kpmg.nl/site.asp?id=40378

Learn from the Leaders: reporting.sustainability.com

London Benchmarking Group (LBG): www.lbg-online.net

Portal for Sustainability Reports: www.sustainability-reports.com

SustainAbility: www.sustainability.com

United Nations Conference on Trade and Development (UNCTAD): www.unctad.org

United Nations Environment Programme Finance Initiative (UNEP FI) Sustainability Reporting webpage: www.unepfi.org/work_ streams/reporting

20
STAKEHOLDER ENGAGEMENT

By embracing the stakeholder relationships at the core of value creation, executives can move beyond the scandals to a sustainable prosperity that they themselves have created and must continually maintain.

R. EDWARD FREEMAN, author of *Strategic Management: A Stakeholder Approach*

Boards must apply the test of fairness, accountability, responsibility and transparency to all acts or omissions and be accountable to the company but also responsive and responsible towards the company's identified stakeholders.

KING REPORT ON CORPORATE GOVERNANCE IN SOUTH AFRICA (2002)

There has been a shift in the balance of power; activists are no longer entirely dependent on the existing media. Shell learned it the hard way with the Brent Spar, when a lot of information was disseminated outside the regular channels.

SIMON MAY, former Shell Internet Manager

We feel this is a matter of free speech, that people should have the right to put alternative views across and criticise multinationals, especially those [companies] who spend a fortune pushing their own propaganda.

HELEN STEEL, one of the 'McLibel' defendants

Ogoni D
demonstration agai
Shell, Nigeria, Janu
19
© Greenpeace/Tim Lam

Learning to engage, listen and respond positively . . .

The stakeholder concept can be traced back to the 1960s, when Stanford Research Institute used it to aid executive thinking about their organisation's external environment. The idea was then employed and tested by a group of scholars and consultants at The Wharton School, including R. Edward Freeman, who set out the concept in his seminal 1984 book *Strategic Management: A Stakeholder Approach*.

The idea of stakeholder accountability steadily gained ground as a challenge to the prevailing focus on shareholder value. By 1994, the King Report on Corporate Governance in South Africa became the first corporate governance code in the world to incorporate stakeholder consultation as a more inclusive approach to management.

Meanwhile, many multinationals were confronting the rise of powerful stakeholder groups, such as cause-driven charities, social and environmental activists and community-based organisations. The mushrooming of the internet meant that many of these groups could rapidly generate support from around the world, despite limited financial resources.

One of the now classic cases of such stakeholder-driven activism came to prominence in 1994 when two anti-McDonald's campaigners were taken to court and sued for libel. In the David versus Goliath trial that ensued, thousands of inter-

1984 *Strategic Management: A Stakeholder Approach* published

1986 'What's Wrong with McDonald's?' leaflet produced

1994 King Report on Corporate Governance in South Africa released

1994 'McLibel' court case begins

1996 Institute for Social and Ethical Accountability established

1996 McSpotlight website set up

1997 *The Stakeholder Corporation* published

1999 AA1000 Framework launched

2004 Morgan Spurlock's *Super Size Me* documentary released

2005 AA1000 Standard for Stakeholder Engagement launched

national civil society organisations came to the activists' defence, criticising McDonald's for its negative impacts and bullying tactics. Despite clearing itself of some of the charges, the company suffered considerable reputation damage in the process.

McDonald's suffered again in 2004 when Morgan Spurlock criticised the negative health effects of its food through his documentary *Super Size Me*, which went on to win an Academy Award. However, this time the company responded more positively, introducing its Balanced Lifestyles initiative in 2005 as a way to begin addressing stakeholder concerns about health.

McDonald's was by no means the only company struggling to find a way through the maze of stakeholder engagement in the 1990s: Shell during the Brent Spar debacle is just one of many other cases in point. Meanwhile, companies such as The Body Shop and Ben & Jerry's were being held up somewhat controversially as exemplars of the stakeholder approach. This simply highlighted the need for some consensus around what constitutes reasonable stakeholder accountability.

AccountAbility (then the Institute for Social and Ethical Accountability) took up the challenge and, in 1999, launched the AA1000 Framework, followed by the AA1000 Assurance Standard in 2003 and the AA1000 Stakeholder Engagement Standard in 2005. It also broadened the concept to apply to countries through its Responsible Competitiveness Index, first piloted in 2003, and now issued biennially.

Today, the debate about the boundaries of corporate responsibility continues, but stakeholder accountability is widely embraced as essential for businesses wishing to survive and thrive in the 21st century.

McDonald's: 'McLibel' and *Super Size Me*

McLibel

In 1986, a UK environmental campaign group called the London Greenpeace Group published a six-page leaflet called 'What's Wrong with McDonald's? Everything They Don't Want You to Know'.

The leaflet contained accusations of McDonald's complicity in starvation in the Third World, rainforest destruction, negative health impacts (including food poisoning, heart disease and cancer), exploitation of children through advertising, 'torture and murder' of animals, anti-union behaviour and poor employee working conditions.

In 1990, five members of the group were issued a writ by McDonald's for publishing and distributing the leaflet, of which two — Helen Steel and Dave Morris — were tried in June 1994.

The resulting 313-day trial (popularly labelled 'McLibel') became the longest ever in British legal history and ended in June 1997, having heard 180 witnesses and reviewed 40,000 pages of documents and witness statements. The verdict was mixed — some of the allegations about McDonald's business practices were upheld, but Steel and Morris were found guilty of having libelled the company and were ordered to pay £60,000 in damages.

Steel and Morris refused to pay the damages (reduced on appeal to £40,000 in 1999), and in 2000 took their case to the European Court of Justice in Strasbourg, alleging that the original trial breached their human rights to a fair trial and freedom of expression. In February 2005, the Strasbourg judged in their favour and awarded compensation.

According to Gerry McCusker, author of *Talespin: Public Relations Disasters*, the trial cost McDonald's more than £10 million in legal fees.

McLibel: Helen Steel and Dave Morris
Karen Robinson

Super Size Me

Super Size Me is an Academy Award-nominated 2004 documentary film written, produced and directed by as well as starring Morgan Spurlock. Spurlock's film follows a 30-day time period (February 2003) during which he subsists entirely on items purchased exclusively from McDonald's.

He consumed an average of 5,000 kcal (the equivalent of 9.26 Big Macs) per day during the experiment. He gained 24.5 lb (11.1 kg), a 13% body mass increase, and his Body Mass Index rose from 23.2 (within the 'healthy' range of 19–25) to 27 ('overweight'). He also experienced mood swings, sexual dysfunction and liver damage. It took Spurlock 14 months to lose the weight he gained.

In 2005, McDonald's announced a Balanced Lifestyles initiative which involves offering healthier menu options, promoting physical activity and providing more nutritional information to customers about its products.

AA1000 and Responsible Competitiveness Index

AA1000

In 1999, AccountAbility published the AA1000 Framework, an accountability guideline on social and ethical accounting, auditing and reporting, including stakeholder engagement. The original sections of the Framework are being revised and republished as individual standards, comprising the AA1000 Series, including:

- AA1000 Assurance Standard (AA1000AS)
- AA1000 Stakeholder Engagement Standard (AA1000SES)
- AA1000 Purpose and Principles (AA1000PP)
- AA1000 Framework for Integration (AA1000FI)

AA1000AS, launched in 2003 and revised in 2008, deals with the assurance of qualitative and quantitative data and underlying systems that reflect sustainability performance.

AA1000SES, also launched in 2005, is a framework for improving the quality of the design, implementation, assessment, communication and assurance of stakeholder engagement.

AA1000PP, currently under development, will address the need for a systematic, legitimate approach to accountability and the role for standards.

AA1000FI, currently under development, will address the need for organisations to integrate their non-financial accountability practices into their core management processes.

Responsible Competitiveness Index

The first biennial Responsible Competitiveness Index was published in 2003. The 2007 Index included 108 countries (83 in 2005 and 51 in 2003). The list now covers countries that account for 96% of global GDP, and includes 17 least developed countries.

The Index is created from 21 data streams from authoritative sources, clustered into three primary domains:

- Policy drivers, including: Signing and Ratification of Environmental Treaties; Ratification of Basic Workers' Rights; Rigidity of Employment Index; Stringency of Environment Regulation; CO_2 Emissions per Billion Dollars; Private Sector Employment of Women; and Responsible Tax Environment;

- Business action, including: Efficacy of Corporate Boards; Ethical Behaviour of Firms; Wage Equality for Similar Work; Strength of Audit and Accounting Standards; Extent of Staff Training; Ratio of ISO Certification; and Occupational Fatalities; and

- Social enablers, including: Corruption Perception Index; Customer Orientation; Press Freedom; Transparency of Transactions; NGO Membership; Civil Liberties; and Impact of Clean Air and Water on Business Operations.

In 2007, Sweden ranked as the world's most responsibly competitive nation, with Denmark, Finland, Iceland, the UK, Norway, New Zealand, Ireland, Australia and Canada also in the top ten in the Index. Strong performers outside Europe included Chile, South Africa and the Republic of Korea.

Taken together, responsible markets in climate change, gender, human rights and anti-corruption will be worth at least US$750 billion by 2050.

Figure 32 **The AA1000 Process Model**
Source: AccountAbility

BOOKS

R. Edward Freeman, *Strategic Management: A Stakeholder Approach* (Financial Times/Prentice Hall, 1984)

Gerry McCusker, *Talespin. Public Relations Disasters: Inside Stories and Lessons Learnt* (Kogan Page, 2004)

Eric Schlosser, *Fast Food Nation: The Dark Side of the All-American Meal* (Harper Perennial, new edn, 2006)

John Vidal, *McLibel: Burger Culture on Trial* (New Press, 1997)

David Wheeler and Maria Sillanpää, *The Stakeholder Corporation: The Body Shop Blueprint for Maximizing Stakeholder Value* (Financial Times/Prentice Hall, 1997)

Abe J. Zakhem, Daniel E. Palmer and Mary Lyn Stoll, *Stakeholder Theory: Essential Readings in Ethical Leadership and Management* (Prometheus Books, 2007)

REPORTS

A21: Reinventing Accountability for the 21st Century (AccountAbility, 2005; rev. 2008)

AA1000 Assurance Standard (AA1000AS) (AccountAbility, 2003)

AA1000 Stakeholder Engagement Standard (AA1000SES) (AccountAbility, 2003)

Accountability Rating 2008: Key Findings from Annual Study of the World's Largest Companies (AccountAbility and csrnetwork, 2008)

Critical Friends: The Emerging Role of Stakeholder Panels in Corporate Governance, Reporting and Assurance (AccountAbility and UTOPIES, 2007)

McDonald's 2006 Worldwide Corporate Responsibility Report (McDonald's)

The Stakeholder Engagement Manual (AccountAbility, United Nations Environment Programme [UNEP] and Stakeholder Research Associates, 2006)

Stakeholder Engagement: A Good Practice Handbook for Companies Doing Business in Emerging Markets (International Finance Corporation [IFC], 2007)

The State of Responsible Competitiveness 2007 (AccountAbility)

WEBSITES

AccountAbility: www.accountability21.net

The Accountability Rating: www.accountabilityrating.com

Center for Science in the Public Interest: www.cspinet.org

Global Reporting Initiative (GRI): www.globalreporting.org

International Finance Corporation (IFC): www.ifc.org

King Report on Corporate Governance in South Africa: www.iodsa.co.za/king.asp

McDonald's Make Your Own Mind Up webpage: www.makeupyourownmind.co.uk

McDonald's Values webpage: www.crmcdonalds.com/publish/csr/home.html

McSpotlight: www.mcspotlight.org

Conclusion

A book of landmarks is a mixed blessing. By focusing on 'key moments', we can offer vivid insights into our achievements and failures, but we must also acknowledge its limitations.

The landmarks celebrate — or, at least, bring to critical scrutiny — moments of dramatic change. These landmarks are ways in which we can analyse the past and consider the progress we have made on the road to sustainability.

The landmarks are in part the outcomes of our activity — the end results of efforts involving business, government and civil society. But they can also act (and have indeed done so) as a driver of change. These incidents have changed the way people have thought about the world and what they have considered possible to achieve. They have also been an inspiration for action — giving people the sense that change is essential and, perhaps, even possible.

While the landmarks represent key events, decisions, agreements or innovations at a particular moment in time, we hope that this publication has emphasised the importance of understanding their evolution. To take one example from the chapter on codes and standards, each of these approaches to codification has, more or less consciously, built on the thinking of its predecessors and the ways in which the 'authors' had tried to formulate and address the problem they faced. Each of the codes has also built on the experience of people attempting to use these codes in the reality of their organisations.

A landmark should not, then, be considered as an isolated moment in time. But, even with this longer perspective, a danger still lurks. The concern is that a book of landmarks may miss the everyday successes — the hard-fought, unsung battles. This book honours a number of high-profile thought leaders and their innovations, while perhaps rendering more invisible the vast swathe of insider influencers who have helped to change their organisations. These latter stories can easily be missed and yet they can be some of the most potent drivers of change.

The Cambridge Programme for Sustainability Leadership recognises the importance of these different aspects of the story of sustainability leadership and change. We know from our work with senior executives of the need to inspire with case studies of personal leadership and practical examples of how transformation can occur. But we also know that there are many people that have influenced in other quiet ways. This informs the way in which we seek to support leaders that have a position of influence — either from the authority of their position, and/or from their way of working or the power of their ideas.

We recognise the need for organisations and individuals to think through these issues in a closed or secure environment and, on a small exploratory scale, this can occur through participation on our open and customised executive programmes. But our other initiatives which look at the ways in which organisations can influence public policy more widely show the significance of landmark actions. This is why our alumni have valued our contribution in supporting them in driving wider societal change through initiatives such as the Bali and Poznan Communiqués, in which hundreds of global business leaders called for a legally binding UN framework to tackle climate change.

This publication marks the transformation of the Cambridge Programme for Sustainability Leadership itself — after 20 years as the Programme for Industry, we have changed our name to the Cambridge Programme for Sustainability Leadership. This is our landmark. It indicates our ambition to address the sustainability agenda more boldly and clearly, while recognising that the success we seek will come from fostering thousands of personal stories of change and impact.

We expect that many of you will be among the leaders who shape the next 20 years of landmark events for sustainability. And we trust that we will be there to encourage and support you all along the way. The time has never been more apt, nor the need so urgent.

Mike Peirce, *Deputy Director, University of Cambridge Programme for Sustainability Leadership*

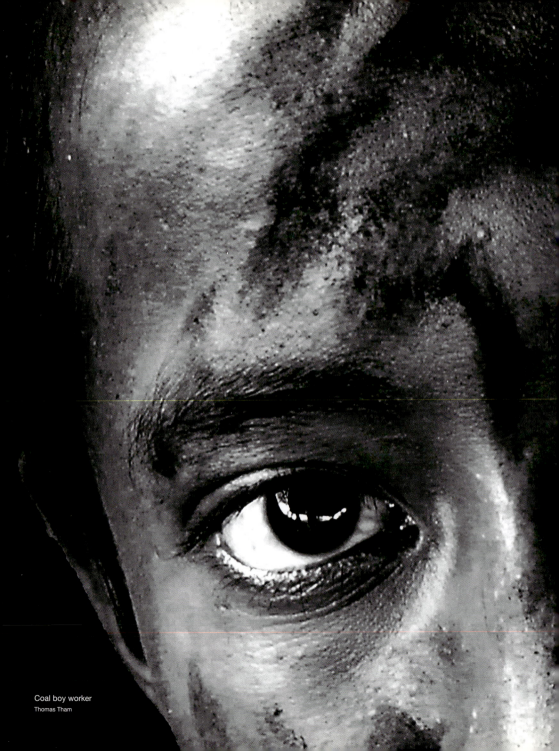

Coal boy worker
Thomas Tham

LANDMARKS
TIMELINE

944	▶ Bretton Woods Conference held in New Hampshire	▶ (Anti-)globalisation, global leadership
945	▶ International Bank for Reconstruction and Development (IBRD) formed	▶ Poverty and development
	▶ United Nations (UN) formed	▶ Global leadership
946	▶ CARE International founded	▶ Poverty and development

Date	Landmark event	Theme
1975	▶ First World Economic (G7) Summit in Rambouillet	▶ (Anti-)globalisation
1976	▶ Chemical explosion at ICMESA chemical plant near Seveso (Italy)	▶ Disaster impacts
	▶ Club of Rome formed	▶ Global leadership
1977	▶ ILO Convention on Occupational Hazards issued	▶ Human rights
	▶ Sullivan Principles launched	▶ Responsible investment
1978	▶ Germany launches the Blue Angel eco-label	▶ Ethical consumerism
	▶ UN Conference on Human Settlements (Habitat I) in Vancouver	▶ World summits
1979	▶ First World Climate Conference	▶ Climate change
	▶ Three Mile Island nuclear power plant accident in the USA	▶ Disaster impacts
1980	▶ Ashoka founded	▶ Business associations
1981	▶ ILO Convention on Occupational Safety and Health issued	▶ Health and safety
1982	▶ Business in the Community founded	▶ Business associations
	▶ Union Carbide gas leak in Bhopal (India)	▶ Disaster impacts
1983	▶ Grameen Bank registered as an independent bank	▶ Social enterprise
1984	▶ FUNDES created	▶ Social enterprise
	▶ *State of the World* first published by Worldwatch Institute	▶ State of the planet
	▶ *Strategic Management: A Stakeholder Approach* published	▶ Stakeholder engagement
1985	▶ Live Aid concerts performed	▶ Poverty and development
	▶ Responsible Care launched	▶ Sector responses

Date	Landmark event	Theme
1986	▶ Chernobyl nuclear plant disaster in the Ukraine	▶ Disaster impacts
	▶ Sandoz chemical spill into Rhine River in Basel (Switzerland)	▶ Disaster impacts
	▶ 'What's Wrong with McDonald's?' leaflet produced	▶ Stakeholder engagement
	▶ *World Resources* first published by World Resources Institute	▶ State of the planet
1987	▶ ISO 9000 standards on quality management published	▶ Codes and standards
1988	▶ Intergovernmental Panel on Climate Change (IPCC) established	▶ Climate change
	▶ Max Havelaar Foundation launch world's first fairtrade coffee	▶ Ethical consumerism
	▶ *Green Consumer Guide* published	▶ Ethical consumerism
1989	▶ *Ethical Consumer* magazine launched in the UK	▶ Ethical consumerism
	▶ *Exxon Valdez* oil spill off Alaskan coast	▶ Disaster impacts
	▶ Rainforest Alliance launches SmartWood certification	▶ Ethical consumerism
1990	▶ First IPCC report finds 0.5° warming	▶ Climate change
	▶ Domini 400 Social Index launched in the USA	▶ Responsible investment
	▶ UN Human Development Index (HDI) launched	▶ Poverty and development
1991	▶ Café Direct founded	▶ Social enterprise
	▶ Petrobras P36 oil platform sinks off Brazilian coast	▶ Disaster impacts
	▶ UK Social Investment Forum (UKSIF) established	▶ Responsible investment
1992	▶ UN Environment Programme (UNEP) Banking Initiative formed	▶ Sector responses
	▶ Business for Social Responsibility (BSR) founded	▶ Business associations

Date	Landmark event	Theme

1992
- ▶ Cadbury Report issued in the UK — ▶ Corporate governance
- ▶ UN Conference on Environment and Development held in Rio de Janeiro — ▶ Global leadership, world summits
- ▶ UNEP's Statement by Banks launched — ▶ Ethical finance
- ▶ UN Framework Convention on Climate Change (UNFCCC) signed — ▶ Climate change
- ▶ *Vital Signs* first published by Worldwatch Institute — ▶ State of the planet

1993
- ▶ Eco-Management and Audit Scheme (EMAS) enacted by the EU — ▶ Codes and standards
- ▶ Forest Stewardship Council (FSC) established — ▶ Sector responses
- ▶ ILO Convention on Prevention of Major Industrial Accidents issued — ▶ Health and safety
- ▶ KPMG launches international survey of environmental reporting — ▶ Sustainability reporting
- ▶ Transparency International founded — ▶ Corruption and transparency
- ▶ UN World Conference on Human Rights in Vienna — ▶ World summits
- ▶ UNEP/SustainAbility issue environmental reporting study — ▶ Sustainability reporting

1994
- ▶ General Agreement on Tariffs and Trade (GATT) signed in Marrakech — ▶ (Anti-)globalisation
- ▶ Green Globe standard for travel and tourism launched — ▶ Sector responses
- ▶ King Report issued in South Africa (revised in 2002) — ▶ Corporate governance
- ▶ London Benchmarking Group established — ▶ Sustainability reporting
- ▶ 'McLibel' court case begins — ▶ Stakeholder engagement
- ▶ UN International Conference on Population and Development in Cairo — ▶ World summits

1995
- ▶ Second IPCC report predicts significant socioeconomic impacts — ▶ Climate change
- ▶ CSR Europe founded — ▶ Business associations
- ▶ International Corporate Governance Network established — ▶ Corporate governance

Date	Landmark event	Theme
1995	▶ Nigerian government executes human rights activist Ken Saro-Wiwa	▶ Human rights
	▶ Shell Brent Spar and Nigeria crises	▶ Disaster impacts
	▶ Transparency International's Corruption Perceptions Index (CPI) released	▶ Corruption and transparency
	▶ UNEP Statement by the Insurance Sector launched	▶ Ethical finance
	▶ World Industry Council on the Environment (WICE) publishes guidelines for voluntary environmental reporting	▶ Sustainability reporting
	▶ World Business Council for Sustainable Development (WBCSD) created	▶ Business associations
	▶ World Summit for Social Development in Copenhagen	▶ World summits
	▶ World Trade Organisation (WTO) established	▶ (Anti-)globalisation
1996	▶ Institute for Social and Ethical AccountAbility established	▶ Stakeholder engagement
	▶ ISO 14001 environmental management standard launched	▶ Codes and standards
	▶ McSpotlight website set up	▶ Stakeholder engagement
	▶ UNAIDS established	▶ Human rights
	▶ UN Declaration Against Bribery and Corruption adopted	▶ Corruption and transparency
	▶ World Food Summit in Rome	▶ World summits
1997	▶ Fair Labor Association Workplace Code of Conduct launched	▶ Human rights
	▶ Fairtrade standard launched internationally	▶ Business associations
	▶ Forum Empresa established	▶ Business associations
	▶ *Global Environment Outlook* first published by UNEP	▶ State of the planet
	▶ Kyoto Protocol sets targets for 34 major economies	▶ Climate change
	▶ International Fairtrade Mark launched	▶ Ethical consumerism
	▶ Marine Stewardship Council (MSC) established	▶ Sector responses

Date	Landmark event	Theme
1997	▶ SA8000 standard on social accountability published	▶ Codes and standards
	▶ Social Venture Network founded	▶ Codes and standards
	▶ *The Stakeholder Corporation* published	▶ Stakeholder engagement
	▶ TRAC Report accuses Nike of labour rights abuses in Vietnam	▶ Human rights
	▶ UNEP Insurance Industry Initiative (III) formed	▶ Sector responses
	▶ UN Human Poverty Index (HPI) launched	▶ Poverty and development
1998	▶ Combined Code issued in the UK (updated in 2003 and 2006)	▶ Corporate governance
	▶ Ethical Trading Initiative established	▶ Ethical consumerism
	▶ International Labour Organisation (ILO) Declaration on Fundamental Principles and Rights at Work adopted	▶ Human rights
	▶ ISO 14020 on environmental labelling launched	▶ Ethical consumerism
	▶ *Living Planet Report* first published by WWF	▶ State of the planet
	▶ Multilateral Agreement on Investment (MAI) abandoned	▶ (Anti-)globalisation
	▶ Oil pipeline explosion at Jesse (Nigeria)	▶ Disaster impacts
	▶ Schwab Foundation for Social Entrepreneurship created	▶ Social enterprise
	▶ UNCTAD issues environmental accounting and reporting guidelines	▶ Sustainability reporting
	▶ World Resources Institute (WRI)/WBCSD Greenhouse Gas Protocol launched	▶ Sustainability reporting
1999	▶ AA1000 Framework standard on accountability published	▶ Codes and standards
	▶ Cement Sustainability Initiative initiated	▶ Sector responses
	▶ Commonwealth Corporate Governance (CACG) Guidelines issued	▶ Corporate governance
	▶ Dow Jones Sustainability Index launched in the USA	▶ Responsible investment
	▶ OHSAS 18001 standard on occupational health and safety published	▶ Codes and standards, health and safety

Date	Landmark event	Theme
1999	▶ Skoll Foundation created	▶ Social enterprise
	▶ WTO protests in Seattle	▶ (Anti-)globalisation
2000	▶ Carbon Disclosure Project launched	▶ Ethical finance
	▶ Environmental Sustainability Index first published	▶ State of the planet
	▶ Global Alliance for Vaccines and Immunisation launched	▶ Health and safety
	▶ Global Reporting Initiative (GRI)'s Sustainability Reporting Guidelines launched	▶ Sustainability reporting
	▶ Kimberley Process to stop trade in conflict diamonds initiative launched	▶ Sector responses
	▶ Mining and Minerals for Sustainable Development (MMSD) project started	▶ Sector responses
	▶ UN Global Compact launched	▶ Business associations
	▶ UN Millennium Development Goals (MDGs) launched	▶ Poverty and development
	▶ UN Millennium Summit in New York	▶ World summits
	▶ Voluntary Principles on Security and Human Rights launched	▶ Human rights
2001	▶ Third IPCC report shows rising temperatures and sea levels	▶ Climate change
	▶ African Institute for Corporate Citizenship (AICC) founded	▶ Business associations
	▶ Enron files for bankruptcy in the US	▶ Corporate governance
	▶ European Social Investment Forum (Eurosif) established	▶ Responsible investment
	▶ First World Social Forum in Porto Alegre	▶ (Anti-)globalisation, global leadership
	▶ FTSE4Good Index launched in the UK	▶ Responsible investment
	▶ G8 Summit protests in Genoa	▶ (Anti-)globalisation
	▶ Global Business Coalition on HIV/AIDS established	▶ Health and safety
	▶ Global Fund to Fight AIDS, Tuberculosis and Malaria set up	▶ Health and safety
	▶ South African Government versus Big Pharma court case	▶ Health and safety

Date	Landmark event	Theme
2002	▶ Arthur Andersen surrenders its CPA licence and goes out of business	▶ Corporate governance
	▶ 'Bottom of the Pyramid' concept introduced by Hart and Prahalad	▶ Poverty and development
	▶ Business Principles for Countering Bribery launched	▶ Corruption and transparency
	▶ Publish What You Pay Campaign launched	▶ Corruption and transparency
	▶ Sarbanes–Oxley Act promulgated in the US	▶ Corporate governance
	▶ Social Enterprise Alliance formed	▶ Social enterprise
	▶ UK government launches a Social Enterprise Strategy	▶ Social enterprise
	▶ WorldCom files for bankruptcy in the US	▶ Corporate governance
	▶ World Summit on Sustainable Development (WSSD) held in Johannesburg	▶ World summits
	▶ London Principles launched at WSSD	▶ Ethical finance
2003	▶ AA1000 Assurance Standard launched	▶ Sustainability reporting
	▶ Carbon Disclosure Project (CDP) launched	▶ Responsible investment
	▶ Equator Principles launched (revised in 2006)	▶ Ethical finance
	▶ Extractive Industries Transparency Initiative (EITI) launched	▶ Corruption and transparency
	▶ Parmalat financial scandal in Europe	▶ Corporate governance
	▶ Roundtable on Sustainable Palm Oil created	▶ Sector responses
	▶ Transparency International's Global Corruption Barometer launched	▶ Corruption and transparency
	▶ UN Convention against Corruption adopted	▶ Corruption and transparency
	▶ UNEP Finance Initiative created	▶ Ethical finance
2004	▶ Anti-corruption added as tenth principle of UN Global Compact	▶ Corruption and transparency
	▶ CSR Asia founded	▶ Business associations

Date	Landmark event	Theme
2004	▸ First UN Global Compact Leaders Summit held in New York	▸ Global leadership
	▸ First Young Global Leaders Award announced	▸ Global leadership
	▸ Gas explosion in Daping coal mine in Henan province in China	▸ Disaster impacts
	▸ JSE Socially Responsible Investment Index launched in South Africa	▸ Responsible investment
	▸ Morgan Spurlock's *Super Size Me* documentary released	▸ Stakeholder engagement
	▸ UN Norms on Business and Human Rights launched	▸ Human rights
	▸ World Bank Extractive Industries Review completed	▸ Ethical finance
2005	▸ AA1000 Standard for Stakeholder Engagement launched	▸ Stakeholder engagement
	▸ Business and Human Rights Resource Centre launched	▸ Human rights
	▸ Corporate Leaders Group on Climate Change issues first open letter	▸ Global leadership
	▸ EU GHG Emissions Trading Scheme begins trading	▸ Climate change
	▸ International Year of Microcredit	▸ Stakeholder engagement
	▸ Live 8 and Make Poverty History campaign	▸ (Anti-)globalisation, poverty and development
	▸ Millennium Ecosystem Assessment published	▸ State of the planet
2006	▸ Environmental Performance Index first published	▸ State of the planet
	▸ ISO 14064 standard on GHG accounting and verification launched	▸ Codes and standards
	▸ Muhammad Yunus and Grameen Bank awarded Nobel Peace Prize	▸ Social enterprise
	▸ Stern Review on Economics of Climate Change published	▸ Climate change
	▸ Transparency International's Bribe Payers' Index launched	▸ Corruption and transparency

Date	Landmark event	Theme
2006	▶ UN Principles for Responsible Investment (PRI) launched	▶ Ethical finance
	▶ Wal-Mart commits to MSC fish stocks and organic cotton	▶ Ethical consumerism
2007	▶ Fourth IPCC report shows 90% certainty of human cause of climate change	▶ Climate change
	▶ Bali Communiqué issued, with 150 global business leaders calling for a legally binding UN framework to tackle climate change	▶ Climate change
	▶ ClimateWise Principles for insurance launched	▶ Ethical finance
	▶ UNEP Declaration on Climate Change issued	▶ Ethical finance
2008	▶ Barack Obama wins the US election, promising wide-scale policy reforms on climate change	▶ Global leadership
	▶ Bill Gates introduces the concept of 'creative capitalism' at the World Economic Forum in Davos	▶ World summits
	▶ US 'credit crunch' turns into a global financial crisis, with banks implicated in irresponsible practices	▶ Ethical finance
	▶ Poznan Communiqué issued, with 140 global business leaders uniting behind the key elements of an international deal on climate change	▶ Climate change

About the author

Wayne Visser is Founder and CEO of CSR International and the author/editor of seven books, including five on the role of business in society, the most recent of which are *Making a Difference* (VDM, 2008) and *The A to Z of Corporate Social Responsibility* (John Wiley, 2007).

In addition, Wayne is a Visiting Professor in CSR at Mannheim University (Germany) and Senior Associate and Internal Examiner at the University of Cambridge Programme for Sustainability Leadership, where he previously held positions as Research Director and External Examiner.

Before getting his PhD in Corporate Social Responsibility (Nottingham University, UK), Wayne was Director of Sustainability Services for KPMG and Strategy Analyst for Capgemini in South Africa.

His other qualifications include an MSc in Human Ecology (Edinburgh University, UK) and a Bachelor of Business Science in Marketing (Cape Town University, South Africa).

Wayne lives in London, UK, and enjoys art, writing poetry, spending time outdoors and travelling in his home continent of Africa. His personal website is www.waynevisser.com.

Research associate

Oliver Dudok van Heel is passionate about finding solutions to the sustainability challenges we face as a society. He believes that by bringing together human ingenuity with respect for our wonderful planet and its people we can develop solutions and create a planet worth living for.

He tries to make this vision reality in different ways. Oliver founded Living Values to help integrate sustainability within corporations. He is a tutor on the University of Cambridge's Postgraduate Certificate on Sustainable Business and a facilitator of the Be The Change Symposium. He helped launch the Lewes Pound, a local currency, to support the local community and reduce its carbon footprint, as part of the Transition Towns movement. He is also a co-founder of Transition Training and Consulting.

Oliver speaks English, French, Dutch, German, Spanish and Portuguese and holds a Master's of Law and an Insead MBA.

Oliver lives in Sussex with his wife and three children.

About CPSL

The University of Cambridge Programme for Sustainability Leadership (CPSL) works with business, government and civil society to deepen the understanding of those who shape the future and help them respond creatively and positively to sustainability challenges.

Our focus on deepening understanding of sustainability through seminars, leadership groups and practical engagement builds on the University's strengths as one of the world's premier academic institutions. Our programmes provide opportunities for leaders to explore and debate key social and environmental trends and their significance within the global economic and political context. We draw on the intellectual breadth of the University and on leading thinkers and practitioners from around the world to help participants examine the array of strategic risks and opportunities and make decisions on the basis of a real appreciation of cutting-edge science, world-class thinking and best practice in business and government.

Our programmes include flagship initiatives inspired by the vision of our Patron, HRH The Prince of Wales. This unique coalition between the University and His Royal Highness gives the Cambridge Programme for Sustainability Leadership the power to convene thought leaders and top-level decision-makers from across the world in order to advance innovative thinking and transformational change.

www.cpsl.cam.ac.uk

We are beginning to realise that whatever we do to Nature — whether it is on the grandest scale or just in our own gardens — is ultimately something that we are doing to our own deepest selves.

HRH Prince of Wales